Ceredigion
40 Coast & Country Walks

The author and publisher have made every effort to ensure that the information in this publication is accurate, and accept no responsibility whatsoever for any loss, injury or inconvenience experienced by any person or persons whilst using this book.

published by
pocket mountains ltd
The Old Church, Annanside, Moffat,
Dumfries and Galloway DG10 9HB
www.pocketmountains.com

ISBN: 978-1-9070254-19

Introduction

The great curve of Cardigan Bay is a little like a bow held at the moment just before an arrow is loosed. If it were a bow, the bowstring would be around 75km (46 miles) long, stretching from Bardsey Island in the north to the landmark hill at Mwnt. When conditions are right you can stand on that hill and see all the way to Bardsey on the far horizon.

Rather than attempting to span the whole bay – which is fringed by the Welsh counties of Gwynedd to the north and Pembrokeshire to the far south – this guide instead covers the beautiful southern portion that falls within Ceredigion. For the purposes of this volume, the northern limit is the estuary of the Dyfi, which has been a frontier of sorts for almost 2000 years and is now the northern boundary of the county. Ceredigion is a relatively new designation which, however, follows the old county borders with an even older name.

In the early 1970s, what was then Cardiganshire became part of a larger administrative area whose name, Dyfed, was borrowed from a Dark Ages kingdom. Modern Dyfed was scrapped in 1996 and the old county was restored, but the council chose to re-invent itself under another ancient name – Ceredigion. The county's name derives from Ceredig, a 6th-century prince from Lothian who was invited to Wales during a time of great crisis. The kingdom that he created was ruled by his descendants for centuries.

Throughout its history, Ceredigion has been something of a battleground and you'll find plenty of reminders of conflict. Iron Age enclosures top many of the hills and Roman forts are a marker of a time when legionaries marched to the outer edge of their world. There are lots of medieval castles too – some built for Welsh princes, others for Norman invaders.

Today, Ceredigion is a county where farming and forestry are major employers. It is the least populated county in Wales after Powys, with about 43 people per sq km (compared to Cardiff, at 4263). All this means that you will find plenty of space to walk in.

The sparsity of population, as well as the variety of habitats, also contributes to its reputation among wildlife-watchers. Most famous for its marine wildlife, Cardigan Bay is one of the best places in Britain to see bottlenose dolphins, including on the New Quay Head walk. A number of species usually confined to warmer waters have also been found here, including Leatherback turtles and Portuguese Man of War jellyfish, while Atlantic grey seals may be spied surfacing near the shoreline or, on the Gwbert and Cwmtydu walks, basking on the rocks. On land, oakwoods are home to pine martens and songbirds, such as the pied flycatcher, and in the uplands you're almost certain to see red kites gliding in the distance.

Using this guide

This guide contains forty routes in Ceredigion, ranging in length from 1km to 15km. The walks featured here are not intended to test the serious hillwalker, but have instead been selected to be as family-friendly as possible, with some routes suitable for wheelchairs and all-terrain buggies – these are highlighted in the text. The recommended time for each walk is a rough estimate based on an average speed of 4kmph, with an allowance added in for ascent and the type of terrain.

Although the Gulf Stream brings warmer temperatures than might be expected at this latitude, it pays to be prepared for some challenging weather – whatever the season. A waterproof jacket and some extra warm layers are always advisable so that you can enjoy these walks in almost any weather. Good walking boots are advisable for all routes.

Some routes follow cliff edges, and care should always be taken when accompanied by children near water or cliffs and gorges. Weather warnings should never be ignored, and even in fine weather the sea can be unpredictable. It pays to keep a safe distance from the water and to know your tide times before you set out on any coastal route.

Mapping

The outline map accompanying each walk is designed to help in planning your trip rather than as a navigational aid: the relevant Ordnance Survey Explorer 1:25,000 map is recommended for most routes.

Six OS Explorer maps will cover all of the routes in this guide, and of these OS Explorer 198 will meet your needs for all of the walks between Cardigan and Aberaeron in the first two chapters, while OS Explorer 213 covers most of the routes in the Aberystwyth and the Rheidol and the North of Aberystwyth chapters. OS Explorer 185, 187 and 199, and OL23 are required for the few routes not covered by the above two maps.

Ceredigion is home to a number of established linear routes – the best-known being the Ceredigion Coast Path, and this guidebook cherrypicks some of its highlights. It has now become part of the Wales Coast Path (which it pre-dates), so its waymarking uses the logos of both. Navigation on these waymarked coastal routes is straightforward enough, but a map is still recommended should you wander off-route.

Public transport

The main towns in this guide can all be accessed by bus, as can most of the villages covered. The excellent Cardi Bach coastal bus between Cardigan and New Quay is a particular gem; it runs each way every day of the week during the summer (from 1st May) and on Thursdays, Fridays and Saturdays from the end of September to the end of April, making it possible to explore the Wales Coast Path on foot while making your return journeys by bus.

It stops at villages along its back road route, but is also a 'hail and ride' service, so you can get on and off anywhere along the way (as long as it is safe for the bus to stop). The Cardi Bach bus is operated by Brodyr Richards, www.richardsbros.co.uk

Elsewhere bus provision is patchy, as it is in most of rural Britain. Most of these walks can be accessed by bus, but in more out-of-the-way locations services may be available only on one or two days a week.

For these reasons, it is best to check timetables when you are planning your day. The Welsh government's Traveline Cymru service is the definitive source for bus information, either online at www.traveline-cymru.info or over the phone on 0871 200 22 33.

Access
Since the Countryside and Rights of Way Act 2000 (CRoW) around one fifth of Wales has been 'access land', which means the public have a right of access on foot. It is mostly open country – moorland, mountains and commons. Ceredigion has large areas of access land, mostly in the uplands of the eastern part of the county. It is clearly marked on OS maps.

The county has a very good network of footpaths and other public rights of way. The Wales Coast Path is very well maintained and signposted as are many other routes, especially those that link with the coast path.

If you are walking with dogs do keep them on a lead if you are near livestock. Also, take care if you are crossing beaches with a dog between late August and October as there can be seal pups along the foot of cliffs and in caves.

Language
Ceredigion is a stronghold of Cymraeg, the Welsh language. In all of Wales about 20 per cent of the population speak the language, but in Ceredigion that figure rises to 47 per cent.

Sounds
C is always hard, like the c in cat
Ch is like the ch in a Scottish loch
Dd is like the th in the
F is like v in violin
Ff is like the ff in off
Ll is easy; just place your tongue as though you're going to say lord and then blow
R is like the r in red, but rolled
Rh place your tongue to say the r in red and then blow

Try . . .
Bore da (Boh-reh dah): Good morning
Prynhawn da (Prin-houn dah): Good afternoon
Iechyd da (Yeh-kid dah): Cheers
Diolch (Dee-olk): Thanks
Nos da (Nohs dah): Good night

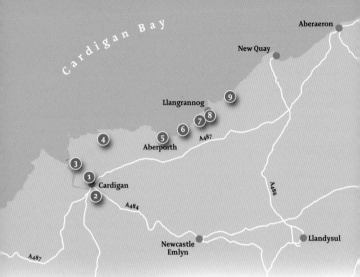

The map shows Cardigan Bay with locations: Aberaeron, New Quay, Llangrannog (9), (8), (7), (6), Aberporth (5), (4), A487, (3), (1) Cardigan, (2), A484, Newcastle Emlyn, Llandysul, A486, A487.

The coastline of Wales is world-class, and the dramatic landscape of wild cliffs and sandy beaches between Cardigan and the village of Llangrannog has to be one of its most beautiful stretches.

As a base for an exploration of Ceredigion's southern coast, the old town of Cardigan is perfect. In the days when Welsh princes slugged it out with Norman warlords Cardigan's bridge over the Teifi was a prize worth the fight. And there was plenty of fighting, with control of the castle changing hands a time or two. The Russian cannon at the Guildhall is a reminder of a more recent conflict – it saw action in the Charge of the Light Brigade during the Crimea War (the brigade was commanded by the 7th Earl of Cardigan).

To the north and east of Cardigan cliffs face the sea, but there are a few small beaches that are well worth a visit. The best-known coastal landmark is the tiny whitewashed church at Mwnt, which stands in splendid isolation close to the clifftops above a picture-perfect cove.

The church must have been a welcome sight for the medieval pilgrims trudging their way between the holy island of Bardsey in the north and St David's in the far west, and here they found simple hospitality.

There are attractive beaches at Aberporth, Penbryn and Tresaith too, but the most popular village is Llangrannog. Sea-going schooners were once built on its beach and shipbuilders lived in the cottages that occupy every inch of level ground (as well as some that isn't) in the steep-sided valley.

St Crannog's Statue looks down over Llangrannog ▶

Cardigan to Llangrannog

Cardigan to Mwnt

Distance 8km **Time** 3 hours 30 (one way)
Terrain field paths and green lanes
Map OS Explorer 198 **Access** bus (T5) from
Aberystwyth to Cardigan; Cardi Bach
coast bus from Mwnt back to the start

**Bring binoculars for this exhilarating
walk from historic Cardigan to the
picturesque cove at Mwnt. Along the way
there's a chance to spot birds on the Teifi
estuary and, if you're lucky, dolphins
around Mwnt cliffs.**

Cardigan is a busy but compact town
and it only takes a minute or two to leave
the bustle for quiet country lanes. Starting
from Greenfield Square car park, head out
of town on Greenfield Row.

Where the lane reaches a driveway gate,

go through a kissing gate to the right to
take the path around the field margin. The
route is well waymarked and in time brings
you to a boatyard.

A metal gate takes you into the yard,
where you pass the main shed before
bearing right down the drive to the
Cardigan-Gwbert road. If you have time,
make a 100m detour to look out over the
Teifi; in winter it's a great place to spot
waders, such as oystercatchers and curlew.

Retrace your steps to pass the boatyard
and, after about 50m, cross the road to a
gate marked 'Bridleway'. The right of way
takes you along the front of a house to a
footbridge. Cross this to go through a
second gate, keeping right to pass a second
house and climb into woodland. The

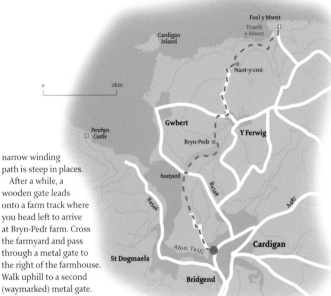

0   2km

narrow winding
path is steep in places.

After a while, a
wooden gate leads
onto a farm track where
you head left to arrive
at Bryn-Pedr farm. Cross
the farmyard and pass
through a metal gate to
the right of the farmhouse.
Walk uphill to a second
(waymarked) metal gate.

Bear north to cross three fields with a
waymarked gate at each hedgerow. After
the last gate the path becomes a track,
which soon joins a country lane.

Go right to the village of Ferwig, turning
left at the welcome sign. The lane winds
past a series of farms for around 1km. After
Ty'r Yet, a house, leave it to take a
waymarked bridleway along the drive of
Nant-y-croi – a farm with campsite. The
bridleway crosses the yard to a green lane
on the left.

Here you're following in the footsteps of
pilgrims towards Foel y Mwnt, the conical
hill ahead. There has been a church at the
foot of this distinctive hill since the 6th

century, and in the Middle Ages it was a
stopping-off point on the pilgrimage from
St David's to Bardsey Island at the end of
the Llyn Peninsula.

After around 500m, the lane comes to a
gate. Keep to the bridlepath towards a lone
cottage, passing its stone wall before
dropping through gorse and bracken to
journey's end – Mwnt seasonal beach café.

Alternatively, for fine views of the coast,
you can detour 1km to Foel y Mwnt: follow
the minor road behind the cove, then cut
across grass to the chapel where, from the
back, a steep path climbs to the summit.

◀ Approaching Mwnt from the west

Teifi Marshes

Distance 3km Time 1 hour 15 (round trip)
Terrain streets, lanes and level gravel
paths Map OS Explorer 198 Access bus (T5)
from Aberystwyth to Cardigan

All the family can enjoy this stroll from
Cardigan to the award-winning Welsh
Wildlife Centre and back. It is perfect for
small children – the path follows a
disused railway line which is easy walking
and buggy-friendly.

Relatively quiet today, Cardigan was once
a major port. In the 1800s many Welsh
emigrants heading for a new life in
America travelled on a Cardigan ship.

Start out from the Quay Car Park at the
bottom of Quay Street. In the port's heyday
the river here would have been busy with
tall-masted sailing vessels, but now only
leisure boats moor in the deeper water.

Walk past the supermarket and up
narrow Quay Street to Bridge Street, just by
the walls of the castle. Invading Normans
built a castle on the Teifi way back in the
1090s (now long gone), but the fortress
you see today is a little younger – it dates
from the early 1100s. Over the years it
changed hands a number of times as
Welsh leaders and the incoming Normans
fought to control the Teifi Valley. For much
of the 12th century it was in the control of
Rhys ap Gruffydd, Prince of Deheubarth;
the first Eisteddfod, a music and poetry
festival, was held at the castle on his
orders in 1176.

Head towards the old bridge and cross
the river using the attached footbridge. On
the far side cross the road towards the

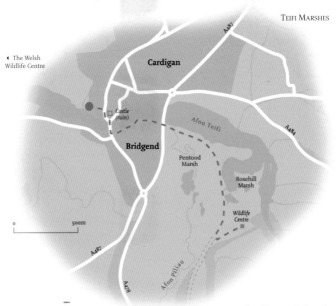

◄ The Welsh
Wildlife Centre

Cardigan

Castle
(ruin)

Afon Teifi

A484

Bridgend

Pentood
Marsh

Rosehill
Marsh

Wildlife
Centre

0   500m

A487

A478

Afon piliau

castle and look for an alley signposted 'River Walk', which is just beyond the pub.

Follow the alley around the pub to a paved riverside path. Along the River Walk you have good views across the water to St Mary's Church, as well as Cardigan Memorial Hospital. This is housed in The Priory, an imposing building designed by the 18th-century architect John Nash, who lived and worked in west Wales in the 1780s and 1790s.

Soon after the trail passes under the Cardigan bypass, you enter Teifi Marshes Nature Reserve and get your first view of its expanse of reedbed, the biggest in Wales. The raised path follows the line of what was once the Whitland and Cardigan Railway, which crossed the wetland on an embankment. Completed in 1885, it closed to passenger traffic in 1962.

Look out along the way for two bird hides on opposite sides of the path. From inside you can look out over open water and there's a good chance of seeing teal and wigeon, a kingfisher or even an otter.

In time the path brings you to a gate. Go through it and turn left into the Wildlife Centre car park. Pass the information board on the left and take the path through the woods to the centre, a striking building of wood and glass that opened in 1993. The centre's restaurant is excellent, with a shop and child-friendly wildlife display. There's also a good children's playground.

Gwbert by the sea

Distance **1km** Time **up to 30 minutes**
Terrain **clifftop paths** Map **OS Explorer 198**
Access **bus (600) from Cardigan to Gwbert**

The plan was that Gwbert would rival
Brighton. As it turned out the Victorian
scheme came to nothing – which means
today's visitor can enjoy the peace and
beauty of a very special stretch of coast.

Stunning views across the mouth of the
Teifi to Poppit Sands and Cemaes Head
on the Pembrokeshire side of the river
are the highlight of this walk, especially
at the end of the day when the sun sets
over the sea.

The route begins at the arched gateway
of the Cliff Hotel, which is a bus stop on
the Cardigan route. If you are arriving by
car, park at the nearby viewpoint on
Coronation Drive (the B4548) and walk to
the hotel.

Gwbert has a long history. Its name

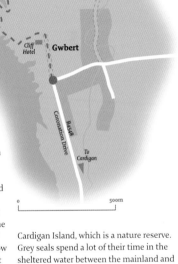

(pronounced 'Goobert') is thought to link Gwbert with St Cubert, an 8th-century missionary who may have stopped off here. Most of the buildings at Gwbert were constructed at the end of the 1800s when a new railway reached Cardigan. Local people saw a chance to cash in by creating a resort at Gwbert 'to challenge Brighton or Scarborough'. An inn was extended and renamed the Cliff Hotel and villas built in readiness for tourists – but little more came of the 'New Brighton' dream.

From the gateway, cross the car park and take the signposted footpath on the far side of the hotel's main building towards the cliff edge. Then bear right to follow the line of the wooden fence around the golf course. The path soon comes to the narrow neck of land that connects Craig y Gwbert to the mainland. A footpath runs around the little peninsula and there's space for one of the golf course's holes too.

Look out for the remaining fragment of the bank that once enclosed an Iron Age fort. The stone building at the cliff edge is much younger; it's a lime kiln, one of many along the Ceredigion coast that prepared limestone for use as a soil improver.

Return over the neck of Craig y Gwbert and go left to follow the cliff path. Ahead is Cardigan Island, which is a nature reserve. Grey seals spend a lot of their time in the sheltered water between the mainland and the island, and can often be seen among the rocks at the bottom of the cliffs.

In time you come to a small C-shaped cove. Skirt above the cove on the cliff path and then look out for a small path to the left which zigzags down to the beach. This can be a bit of a scramble, but it is well worth the effort to reach the sand – a sheltered sun-trap which is perfect for a day that's sunny but breezy. When you've had your fill, retrace your steps to the Cliff.

◄ Looking towards Cardigan Island from the cliffs at Gwbert

Mwnt to Pen Peles

Distance **7km** Time **2 hours 30**
Terrain **coast path, public footpath and
country lane. Some sharp gradients**
Map **OS Explorer 198** Access **Cardi Bach
coast bus from Cardigan to Mwnt**

**With its landmark hill and tiny
whitewashed church, Mwnt is one of the
most photographed Cardigan Bay
locations. Take along a camera and try to
capture its beauty for yourself on this
coast and country circuit.**

The Church of the Holy Cross at Mwnt
dates from the 14th century, but there has
been a church on the site far longer. It is a
peaceful spot, but one with a dark past; in
the 1150s a force of Flemings landed at
Mwnt cove, intending to raid Welsh
territory. The locals turned out to be more
than a match for the raiders, who were
allies of Norman lords who controlled
Pembrokeshire at the time. The Flemings

were 'encountered by the natives, and
repulsed with great slaughter'.

For centuries local people celebrated the
victory on the first Sunday of January,
which they called Sul Coch y Mwnt (The
Bloody Sunday of Mwnt). For the most
part, though, Mwnt has had more spiritual
connections; in the Middle Ages it was on
the coast's pilgrim route.

From the church follow the waymarked
Coast Path east. Looking back at Foel y
Mwnt it's easy to see what a useful
landmark it must have been for pilgrims
because the pyramid-shaped summit
stands well above the surrounding
coastline. The rocks that make up the coast
here are 500 million-year-old shales. Later
movements of the earth's crust have
twisted and shifted the rock layers, which
you can see on the cliff faces.

When the path comes to a valley with a
fast-flowing stream, look for a fingerpost

◀ The Church of the
Holy Cross at Mwnt

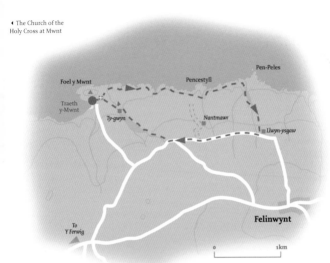

that points the way right. Leaving the Coast Path you climb to enter a wood – it's then a steady ascent until you reach a footbridge and enter a large field.

Follow the stream uphill. In time you arrive at another footbridge and the path passes through a wood to a kissing gate, which opens onto a lane.

Go right, taking a moment to look at the old waterwheel at the roadside. Follow the lane west until you come to a junction, where the route takes you straight ahead on the road signposted 'Mwnt'.

After the second of two bungalows, look for a concrete track marked Graig on the right. Take this bridleway, which soon passes another bungalow and then goes through a farm (keep the farmhouse on your right). Take the marked path from the farmyard. The green lane drops down to a second farm; again follow bridleway signs to pass the house.

Follow the lane up to the church. As you go you will cross what was possibly the battlefield – there is a story that a mass grave was once found 200m southeast of the church. However, the grim story of the massacre does have a partial happy ending. One Fleming survived the battle and is said to have been cared for by a Mwnt girl. In time the pair married and raised a large family. Retrace your steps to the start.

Aberporth to Tresaith

Distance 2.5km Time **1 hour (one way)**
Terrain **roads, paths, cliff edges**
Map **OS Explorer 198** Access **bus (T5) from
Cardigan to Aberporth; Cardi Bach coast
bus from Tresaith back to the start**

**This short hop between two of the coast's
most popular seaside villages is just right
for families. The gradients are untaxing
and the path is an 'Inclusive Access' trail
for three-quarters of the way, which
means it is wheelchair-friendly.**

Until the early 1900s the village of
Aberporth was a busy fishing centre. In the
industry's heyday as many as 20 boats put
out from Aberporth's twin beaches to
chase herring shoals.

Start out from Aberporth's landmark
sculpture, a life-sized dolphin that is a
reminder that Cardigan Bay is home to a
resident community of bottlenose
dolphins. They are often spotted from cliffs
on this stretch of coast. There's plenty of
parking spaces close by, as well as two
cafés if you want to pick up a picnic. Spare
a moment to go up to the nearby look-out
point; on a clear day you can see the peaks
of Snowdonia around 100km (62 miles) to
the north.

From the car park follow the road down

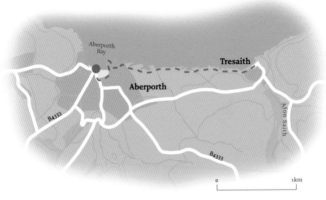

past a pub, The Ship, and over the river, then turn left onto a concrete path that skirts the beach. Walk uphill, keeping to the path. In time the path doubles back on itself, passing a row of cottages. Take the left turn at a house with a metal balcony – look out for the Coast Path fingerpost.

Where the road ends, take an alley that does a dog-leg between houses to bring you to the clifftop. The route ahead is straightforward, following the cliffs all the way to the village of Tresaith, and for most of the journey the path has been surfaced with tarmac. The last quarter of the route is steep and gravelled, which means that wheelchair users have to turn back.

As you walk, look out for the coast's most unusual 'buildings', three old railway carriages that have been converted for use as holiday homes. Soon after the last stretch of the route, you can see the path zigzag down to Tresaith beach.

On the way down, you look across the cove to the village's main landmark, a stream which plummets from the cliffs to the beach below. The scale of the waterfall depends on how much rain has fallen in recent days, but even in a dry summer a trickle drops to the beach. That is perhaps why a German submarine captain called in during World War I to top up his vessel's water tank – the story goes that he had visited Tresaith in peacetime and made a mental note that the cove could be a handy source of freshwater.

Tresaith is the perfect place to while away an hour or two. There's a good beach café and the pub, also called The Ship, has a garden that overlooks the sea.

You can head home back up the zigzag path to Aberporth or take the Cardi Bach coast bus. The return journey by bus takes less than 10 minutes, but services are infrequent so check the timetable first.

◀ Village history mosaic at Aberporth

Thieves' Valley to Penbryn Beach

Distance **2km** Time **1 hour**
Terrain **woodland paths and minor roads**
Map **OS Explorer 198** Access **Cardi Bach coast bus from Cardigan calls at Llanborth**

There's not that much to Penbryn, just a few houses, a tiny church and – arguably – Ceredigion's most beautiful beach. Even better, it is a beach that you walk to, so even in high season it's rarely busy.

This short walk begins at St Michael's Church, which stands on its own on a hill with views of the sea - but hidden from it. In Viking times it didn't pay to catch the attention of passing ships.

If you are arriving by car there's a car park opposite the church, which you can use in

return for an honesty box donation. From here, head down to the church. One interesting feature of St Michael's is its circular Celtic churchyard. Many of Wales' oldest churches stand in circular churchyards – it was said the shape left no corner for the Devil to hide in.

From the church go a little further down the lane and then take a path on the left through a kissing gate. Cross the field to the gate on the far side and go through it into a wood, which covers the valley side.

The valley between the church and the beach is called Cwm Lladron, or Thieves' Valley. It was used by smugglers in the 18th century as a handy hiding place.

Where the path meets another trail, go left to walk uphill. When you leave the

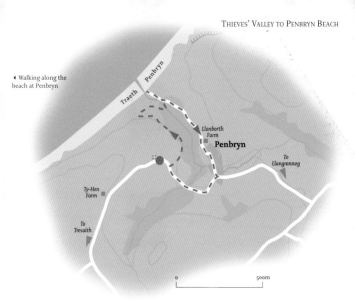

◄ Walking along the beach at Penbryn

wood at the field edge there are fantastic views of the beach. This is a place in Bond film history as it was a location for 2002's *Die Another Day*. Bond (Pierce Brosnan) and Jinx (Halle Berry) were filmed together in a 'temple' that was built on the cliffs.

The path bears to the left and in time brings you to a fingerpost and gate. Don't go through the gate – instead take the narrow path to the right. This takes you down steps to a field. The path follows the line of a clifftop fence to loop back into the valley wood. It then drops down to steps that bring you to a path by a stream. Go left to follow this downstream.

Cross a footbridge and, soon after, you arrive at the beach itself. When you are

ready to return there is a choice of routes. The most direct one is to retrace your steps over the footbridge and take the lower path through the wood to rejoin your outward route just below St Michael's Church.

Alternatively, take the minor road uphill and through Llanborth Farm. For most of the year, there's the option of a tea or coffee at the Cartws café, on the right. Leaving the cafe, take the lane over a bridge to reach a T-junction, where you turn right.

The lane passes an attractive house called Pencwm, which has a link with the architect Clough Williams-Ellis (of Portmeirion fame). He masterminded a makeover of the house in the 1920s for his brother. From Pencwm the lane climbs steeply to bring you back to St Michael's.

Penbryn to Llangrannog

Distance 5.5km **Time** 3 hours **Terrain** coast path with steps in places, woodland paths and minor roads **Map** OS Explorer 198 **Access** Cardi Bach coast bus from Cardigan to Llanborth, Penbryn

Llangrannog is one of Ceredigion's best-loved seaside villages and the coast to the south is spectacular. This route makes a great day out, combining breathtaking scenery with a chance of an ice cream on the beach.

This walk starts at the car park and café at Llanborth, which is also a stop on the coast bus route. Go past the farmhouse and along the lane towards the sea, but leave the road when you come to a bridleway on the right.

Head towards a wooded hill and at a T-junction of paths go right. The route soon reaches a large house, passing through woodland to the rear.

At a fork, go left. It is then a long, steady climb to a gate that opens onto a green lane. Follow the lane until it comes to a minor road and go left. When you come to a junction take the lane on the left. At a farm called Morfa Isaf go past the farmhouse and then look for a path on your right.

Pass through a metal gate to make for the stile ahead of you. After climbing over the stile, drop downhill with the hedge on your left.

On the far side of the field look for a gap in the hedge that opens into a second field. Walk on, aiming for the v-shape of the valley in the cliffs ahead.

As you reach bushes you'll see a fence on

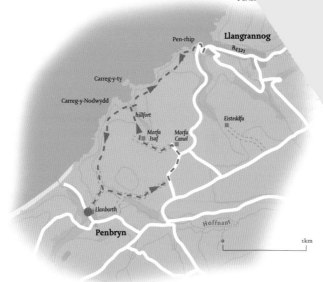

Llangrannog

Pen-rhip

B4321

Carreg-y-ty

Carreg-y-Nodwydd

hillfort

Morfa Isaf

Morfa Canol

Eisteddfa

Llanborth

Hoffnant

Penbryn

0   1km

your right. Keep following the path, which bears left to reach another stile. Climb over the stile and keep going downhill until the path joins the Coast Path at Traeth Bach. Go right to cross a stream on a footbridge and it's then a muscle-testing climb up to a plateau. Look at the landforms around you here – you may be able to make out Castell Bach, an Iron Age hillfort.

From Castell Bach it's easy walking on the Coast Path to the statue of Saint Caranog at Pen-rhip. Caranog was a well-travelled 6th-century missionary who lived in seclusion on the cliffs near Llangrannog and also gave his name to villages in Somerset, Cornwall and Brittany.

Leaving Pen-rhip, join the road that zigzags down into the village. Llangrannog is a good place for a lunch stop, with two pubs, a couple of good cafés and a useful village shop. If you can't face the walk back there's the option of catching the coast bus; otherwise retrace your steps to Traeth Bach. Follow the Coast Path towards the telecommunications mast and then go through a gate to follow the trail along the cliffs. At a second gate take a moment to enjoy the marvellous views of Penbryn Beach below, then walk on to a third gate that opens onto a farm track.

This leads downhill where, in time, you rejoin your outward route. Go right downhill and then left on the road at Llanborth.

◀ The landmark Carreg Bica rock just off Llangrannog beach

...nd Pigeonsford

...r roads
... 198 Access **Cardi Bach**
...from Cardigan to Llangrannog
...d from the Patio Café back to the start

The seaside village of Llangrannog is one of the most popular along the Ceredigion coast. This route offers the chance to combine time on the beach with an exploration of the surrounding countryside.

Parking is limited in Llangrannog and can be a problem during high season, so it pays to arrive by bus or to use the larger (and free) car park on the edge of the village.

If you are starting out from the beach take the main road past the village shop, climbing uphill to a junction at the church where you turn right. You soon pass the free car park on the left – your start point if you have arrived by car. Carry on uphill and look for a footpath on the left, close to a tight bend in the road.

The path takes you through woodland and, in time, passes the large country house of Pigeonsford on the left. Soon after, the path crosses a yard surrounded by outbuildings. Walk straight across the yard and on to a minor road. Go left to reach a crossroads, then straight across this.

Look for a footpath on the left that soon brings you to a kissing gate. After passing through the gate, bear right to follow the field boundary.

The nearby buildings in the valley on your right are an activity centre run by the Welsh language youth organisation, Urdd

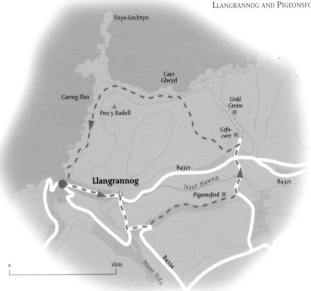

Gobaith Cymru. At the corner of the field go through a gate and cross the middle of the next field to reach a kissing gate. Beyond the gate, bear right towards the sea. At the next fence go through one gate and then left to a second, which is marked 'Coast Path'.

The path soon brings you to a vantage point above the low-lying Lochtyn Peninsula. On a clear day it is possible to make out Bardsey Island on the far side of Cardigan Bay – more than 40 miles away. It is the location that possibly inspired the composer Sir Edward Elgar, who holidayed at Llangrannog in 1901. In a notebook he described walking on the coast and hearing people singing, a moment that

inspired part of his 'Introduction and Allegro for String Orchestra'.

Where the wide track begins to swing inland look for a less-distinct path that bears to the right. It heads down to a path that skirts the base of the hill.

Stay on the path as you bypass the hill to reach a gate on the right, marked 'Coast Path'. Go through this and follow the clifftop path to Llangrannog, which brings you to the top of the beach just by the popular Patio Café – the end of the route if you are using the coast bus. If not, treat yourself to tea and cake (or an ice cream, if the weather is being kind) and then use the first section of the route above to get to your car park.

◄ The Lochtyn Peninsula from the Coast Path

Llangrannog to Cwmtydu

Distance 7.75km Time 3 hours (one way)
Terrain footpaths and tracks; steep steps
to start and a long climb later on
Map OS Explorer 198 Access Cardi Bach
coast bus from Cardigan to Llangrannog,
and from Cwmtydu back to the start

A walk along what is, arguably, the most
impressive stretch of cliff scenery on the
Ceredigion coast – but with the path on a
cliff-edge in places you need a good head
for heights.

Your start point for this coast walk is the
popular Patio Café at the top of
Llangrannog Beach. Next to the café, the
Coast Path climbs steps that rise steeply
out of the cove.

At the top of the cliffs, go straight on to
pass Cilborth Beach and on towards Pen y
Badell, the hill that dominates this stretch
of the coast. Along the way go through one
gate and then straight on to a second.

Go left at the gate towards the Lochtyn
Peninsula. When you come to a bench,
keep left to take the path along the spine
of the headland to its end. The vantage
point above the narrow channel between
the headland and island is good for seal-
spotting, especially in early autumn.

Retrace your steps until you reach a
stone wall that crosses the headland. Here,
go left on a path that takes you around Pen
y Badell's lower slopes. When the path
splits, bear left to climb the slope to a

◀ The cliff path where it climbs
on the way to Cwmtydu

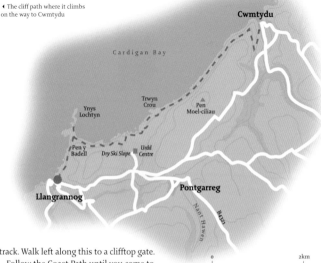

Cwmtydu

Cardigan Bay

Trwyn
Crou

Ynys
Lochtyn

Pen
Moel-ciliau

Pen y
Badell   Dry Ski Slope   Urdd
Centre

Llangrannog   **Pontgarreg**

Nant Hawen

Hescil

0   2km

track. Walk left along this to a clifftop gate.

Follow the Coast Path until you come to the top of a dry ski slope, which is part of an activity centre run by the Welsh-language youth organisation Urdd. Carry on downhill towards an information board close to the centre's boundary fence.

Go left here to follow the fence to a gate next to a stone that marks the opening of the Ceredigion Coast Path in 2008. Further on, at Trwyn Crou, the route brings you to a fingerpost and then the climbing begins – ahead is a long uphill section where the path is cut into the cliff face.

When the path levels out, it follows the line of an old stone wall before dropping down to another fingerpost, where you go right to descend into the valley.

Head straight on at a kissing gate and

then turn left to go through a second kissing gate and carry on downhill. In time you will come to a footbridge. After crossing this, pass some public toilets and walk on to the road through Cwmtydu. Go left to reach the beach.

The coast bus from Cwmtydu takes 20 minutes to get back to Llangrannog. If you would rather return on foot, head back along the village street to the first road junction and go right over a stone bridge.

At the next T-junction go right and then right again just after the gate to the Gilfach caravan park. At the next junction, go right yet again onto a B-road, which in time brings you to Llangrannog.

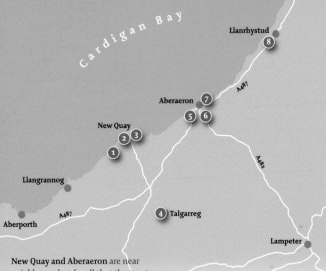

New Quay and Aberaeron are near
neighbours, but for all that the two towns
are very different characters. If you know
Dylan Thomas' 'Under Milk Wood' you'll
have a feel for what makes New Quay tick
because the writer created his fictional
seaside town while he was living just
outside the little fishing town.

His imaginary community, Llareggub,
was a Welsh archetype and New Quay has
a lot in common with his creation. It has
lots of pubs and fish and chip shops and
is a cheerful, busy, gossipy sort of place
that's always fun to spend time in.

Aberaeron is its posher sibling, close
enough to be related but a little more self-
conscious about its standing in the world.
It has great fish and chips too, but the
chip shops are outnumbered by smart
restaurants, such as the award-winning
Harbourmaster Hotel. Aberaeron as it

appears today is comparatively new,
created almost from scratch as a Georgian
new town from the early 1800s, with some
noteworthy architecture.

Geology divides the neighbours too.
New Quay is at a geological boundary that
sees the character of the coast change
dramatically. To the south and west of
New Quay, tall cliffs face up to all that the
sea can throw at them, but from New
Quay to Aberaeron and beyond the
coastline is quite different – low-lying
with big pebbly beaches and cliffs that
seem to erode before your very eyes.

The last of the walks in this section – to
Llanrhystud – takes you north out of this
low-level coastal strip and back to the
hills and cliffs.

Cob statue in Aberaeron ▶

New Quay and Aberaeron

Cwmtydu and Castell Bach

Distance **1.5km** Time **40 minutes**
Terrain **coast paths, steep in places**
Map **OS Explorer 198** Access **Cardi Bach coast bus from Cardigan to Cwmtydu**

The little cove below Castell Bach is one of the most beautiful along this section of coast. It takes a leg-stretching walk from Cwmtydu to get to it, but you'll find the effort is more than repaid.

The short walk to Castell Bach is a joy at any time of year, but is a special treat in late summer and early autumn when seal pups are born on the tiny rocky beaches around Cwmtydu. You may even see them from the Cwmtydu beach car park, which is the start point for this walk.

From the car park, pass the limekiln to reach the Coast Path, which is signposted. The path climbs steeply to a junction at a fingerpost where you take the trail on the left, signposted 'Coast Path'.

This climbs through gorse bushes, with impressive views down into Cwmtydu cove and along the coast to the west. In the 18th century this was smuggler country and Cwmtydu is said to have been one of the locations used by a master smuggler called Siôn Cwilt, who became a local hero in his day.

The remote coast and sheltered beach made the perfect location for landing wines, spirits and other contraband, which Siôn then moved inland as quickly as he could before customs officers could put in an appearance. Why the smuggler

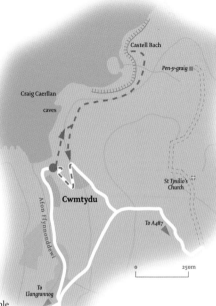

◄ Overlooking the little beach at Castell Bach

was given the nickname Cwilt is open to question; one theory is that it was because he wore a colourful quilted coat.

In time the path leaves Cwmtydu and then begins to drop down towards Castell Bach's clifftop plateau and on to the beach below it. Close to 2500 years of weathering have taken their toll on the Iron Age fort at Castell Bach (Little Castle). Erosion has eaten away at the ground below the fort, but though some of it has been lost to the sea below, it remains an incredible vantage point.

As you get closer you should be able to make out where the cliff edge cuts through the fort enclosure. Free-roaming ponies graze the clifftops around the fort and the close-cropped turf is a favourite with one of the coast's rarer birds, the chough. From a distance, a chough looks like a small crow, but up close you will see that its legs and bill are a striking bubblegum pink. They spend much of their time probing the ground in search of insects.

Follow the path around the cove, looking out for the bank of the hillfort as you go. When the fort was in use it is thought that the defences were topped with a fence of branches or thorn bushes.

The path down to the beach is on the eastern side of the cove. Take care if you climb down – it's quite a scramble.

When it is time to head back, retrace your steps out of the cove and along the Coast Path to the fingerpost, where you now take the left-hand path to leave the coast behind. This soon brings you to a minor road – go right to drop down to your start point.

29

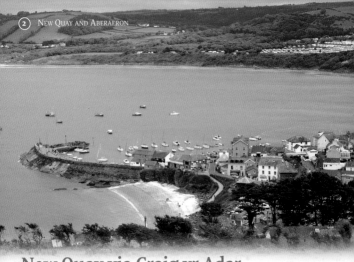

New Quay via Craig yr Adar

Distance **6km** Time **2 hours (one way)**
Terrain **coast paths, steep in places**
Map **OS Explorer 198** Access **Cardi Bach
coast bus from Cardigan to Cwmtydu, and
from Park St, New Quay back to the start**

With steep cliffs and big views, the clifftop
route to New Quay from Cwmtydu is
impressive. Look out along the way for
seabirds and for dolphins, which are often
seen around New Quay Head.

From the beach car park at Cwmtydu
look for the Ceredigion Coast Path, which
leaves the cove just beyond an old
limekiln. It climbs steeply and in a short
time you will be high above the sea.

You soon pass the first of two beaches
only accessible on foot, the little cove
below the Iron Age hillfort of Castell Bach
(Little Castle). The fort has been partly

eaten away over the years by erosion and
you can make out its cut-through rampart
on the cliff face above the sand.

About 500m further on, the path drops
again, this time into the V-shaped valley
of the Afon Soden. A short detour will
take you down to a small beach that you
are very likely to have to yourself – in late
spring it is also one of the few sites in
Wales where you can see the pearl-
bordered fritillary butterfly.

After Cwm Soden the route rises high
above sea level again. When the path
finally reaches the old Coastguard
Lookout, you are around 100m above
where waves break on Craig yr Adar
(Birds Rock). It is a good place to take some time
to scan sea and sky. Look out for gannets,
which often pass close by. With a four-
foot wingspan they are the largest birds

◀ View from the Coast Path above New Quay

you're likely to see and their brilliant white plumage makes them easy to spot. Gannets travel long distances to fish in Cardigan Bay before returning to their nesting colony on Grassholm Island, west of Pembrokeshire.

In spring and early summer there's also a chance to spot razorbills, which nest on the cliffs below the lookout. Razorbills look a little like penguins – they are dark chocolate brown and white with small wings. You'll often see them in groups resting on the sea.

The stretch of coast between New Quay and Cardigan Island is an important feeding ground for bottlenose dolphins

and, as a result, is protected as a Special Area of Conservation. The lookout is used for dolphin monitoring.

Leaving the lookout, keep left to take the cliff edge path. Where this reaches the edge of town pass a row of bungalows and then look for a fingerpost (marked 'Coast Path') on the left. Follow this left along a narrow path that drops down to a minor road.

At the road go left. It soon ends at an area of grass above the town's fish factory. From here, bear right to pass a waymark post and then head to a kissing gate, which opens onto Rock Street.

Walk along Rock Street, passing its colourful terraced houses, to eventually pass the tourist information centre and arrive at the end of the walk, New Quay Harbour.

New Quay or Llareggub?

Distance **1.5km** Time **30 minutes**
Terrain **town roads** Map **OS Explorer 198**
Access **bus (50) from Aberystwyth to
New Quay**

Once a shipbuilding centre, New Quay is
now one of Ceredigion's most popular
seaside resorts and is said to have inspired
Dylan Thomas in the creation of his best-
known work, 'Under Milk Wood'.

It is hard to say which of Dylan Thomas'
works has had the biggest impact, but his
play for radio 'Under Milk Wood' has to be
a contender. It is set in an archetypal
Welsh seaside town called Llareggub and
no-one can say for sure which town he
had in mind for his 'warts and all' portrait
of a small community.

Exploring New Quay you follow in

Thomas' footsteps, and you'll see his face
on blue plaques at key locations around
the town. Start on Church Street by the
junction with Hill Street; it is near a bus
stop and New Quay's largest car park.

Head uphill along Church Road and
turn left onto Towyn Road where you'll
soon pass Wendowel on the right, a
house which once belonged to Thomas'
aunt Elizabeth.

Continue along Towyn Road to arrive at
a junction with Park Street and Margaret
Street. Go right to follow Margaret Street,
carrying straight on as it becomes George
Street to reach a viewpoint with benches
on the left. The closest headland across
the bay is Llanina Point, where Thomas'
family lived in the 1940s when he was
working on 'Under Milk Wood'. At Llanina

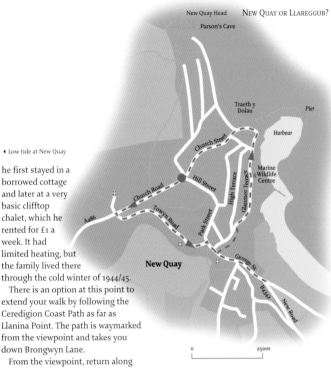

Parson's Cave

Traeth y Dolau

Pier

Harbour

Church Street

Marine Wildlife Centre

Hill Street

High Terrace

Glanmor Terrace

Church Road

A486

Towyn Road

Paul Street

New Quay

George St

B4342

New Road

◀ Low tide at New Quay

he first stayed in a borrowed cottage and later at a very basic clifftop chalet, which he rented for £1 a week. It had limited heating, but the family lived there through the cold winter of 1944/45.

There is an option at this point to extend your walk by following the Ceredigion Coast Path as far as Llanina Point. The path is waymarked from the viewpoint and takes you down Brongwyn Lane.

From the viewpoint, return along George Street as far as the narrow Pilot Lane on your right. Take this lane, which eventually opens onto Glanmor Terrace at the Black Lion Inn, said to have been the poet's favourite pub.

Turn right along Glanmor Terrace, stopping in to visit the Cardigan Bay Marine Wildlife Centre further along on the right. Its exhibition is a great source of information about the Cardigan Bay Special Area of Conservation, which takes in the coast between Aberaeron and the

0   250m

mouth of the Teifi. The area is protected as it is an important feeding ground for bottlenose dolphins. A community of up to 300 live in Cardigan Bay and often visit New Quay Bay.

At the end of Glanmor Terrace, carry on past the tourist information centre and into Glyn Square. Head up Church Street to pass another Dylan Thomas pub, The Dolau Inn. It's now a short walk uphill to reach the junction with Hill Street.

33

Talgarreg

Distance **5km** Time **2 hours**
Terrain **farm paths and country lanes**
Map **OS Explorer 198** Access **no public
transport to the start**

The small village of Talgarreg is
somewhere to get away from it all. That's
possibly why it has attracted well-known
writers; the Welsh language poet Dewi
Emrys retired here (and is buried in
nearby Pisgah) and the great Dylan
Thomas also spent time in the village.

From Talgarreg's church, walk south
until you pass a postbox. Look for the
kissing gate on the right a little further
on, which opens into a field.

Cross the field to a second kissing gate,
go over a footbridge and then bear
diagonally left across a field to an iron

gate. Follow the path to the left and
around the front of a house to a small
gate that opens onto a track. Take this to
reach a minor road and head straight on
to pass to the right of a house.

After 1km of road walking, you will see a
gate on the right marked 'Rhydwen'. Turn
up the track – you'll soon see a farmhouse
in the valley below. Pass the house and
look out for a path on the left just where
the track swings to the right. The path
passes between old gateposts into a field.

Drop downhill to cross a footbridge over
the Nant Glowen and then carry straight
on to a gate. Go through this and aim for
a large tree in the middle of the field,
where a nearby waymark post points to a
gate in the top corner of the field.

Go through the gate and turn left along

◂ The Welsh Independent Chapel, Pisgah

a track. Where the track bears left towards a farm building, leave it to go right.

Follow the hedgeline until you reach a fieldgate on the right. Go through this and aim for the farm ahead, crossing a small footbridge mid-field to reach a gate in front of you. Here, turn right onto a minor road to walk to Pisgah.

As you come into the hamlet look out for a footpath sign just before the chapel. The path on the right passes a house called Sunnyhill. Just beyond the house, go through a gate into a stableyard, passing the front of the stables and continuing to a gate at the corner of a field.

From the gate, keep to the right, then bear left after 150m, cutting a corner to a gate onto a lane. Drop downhill to a farmyard. Go through the double gate ahead and then through a gate on the left. Head straight on to enter a field and bear right towards a gate in its far corner.

After crossing a footbridge, turn left, keeping close to the hedge on your left as you continue. A kissing gate on the far side of the field opens onto a road. A right turn, then right again at the next junction returns you to Talgarreg's main street and, in time, the church.

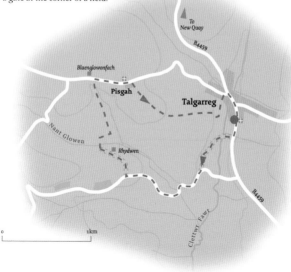

Aberaeron to Henfynyw

Distance **8km** Time **2 hours**
Terrain **field paths and green lanes**
Map **OS Explorer 198** Access **bus (T5) from
Aberystwyth and Cardigan to Aberaeron**

**St David spent his childhood at the village
of Henfynyw, so you'll be walking in the
footsteps of the patron saint of Wales on
this circuit through town and country.**

Begin at the car park at the end of
Wellington Street (Heol yr Odyn). It's on
the southern side of the harbour, a
pebble's throw from the beach.

Leaving the car park, head out of town
along Beach Parade. Where the road ends,
continue to a fingerpost pointing the way
to the Coast Path, which runs close to the
cliff edge, passing two bungalows. In time
it brings you to the Ceri Brook, which
flows through steep-sided Cwm Clifforch.

A footbridge takes you across the water
and the path climbs to a gate, which you
pass through. Bear left when you see
holiday chalets ahead and aim for a
waymark post. At the post, go left to a
kissing gate which opens onto a minor
road.Turn left and, as you approach a gate
across the road after about 500m, look out
for a stile on the left. Cross the stile and
follow the fenceline to a second stile,
which takes you into a small copse of trees.

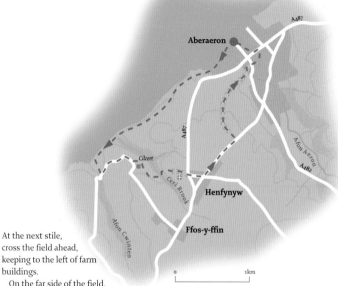

At the next stile, cross the field ahead, keeping to the left of farm buildings.

On the far side of the field, climb a stile into a lane and continue to another stile on the left. Go over this stile and cross to another, which takes you into the wooded Ceri valley. At a footbridge cross the Ceri and follow the path around the perimeter of a paddock.

As you near a house, keep left to follow its drive. This takes you past St David's Church in Henfynyw. Built in the 1860s, it is said to stand on the site of an early monastery. Cross the main road and go up the road opposite (Bro Ddewi).

At the end of Bro Ddewi, turn left where, after a little more than 500m, you'll come to a 'Welcome to Aberaeron' sign. Shortly after this, there is a footpath fingerpost on the left. This path leads you along a hedge bank to a gate and stile. Cross the stile and bear right to join a track.

Stay on this track for about 1km. When it comes to a road, cross straight over into an entry marked 'Craft Centre'. On the right you'll see a fingerpost pointing the way to a public path, which brings you to a path along the banks of the Aeron.

Go left to the roadbridge and then left again at the main road, crossing the road to enter the riverside park. The path through the park bears left and soon brings you to the junction with Beach Parade and your start point.

◀ Leaving Aberaeron

The Aeron Valley to Llanerchaeron

Distance **4km** Time **1 hour 30 (one way)**
Terrain **roads, cycle trail and fields**
Map **OS Explorer 198** Access **bus (T5) from
Aberystwyth and Cardigan to Aberaeron;
hourly bus (40) back to the start**

**Poet Dylan Thomas said the Aeron Valley
was 'the most precious place in the world'
and he could well be right. At any time of
year this buggy-friendly route is a joy.**

Alban Square is the focus of Aberaeron
and the start point for this exploration of
the Aeron Valley. At its southwest corner
you'll find a statue of a Welsh cob, the
traditional horse breed of Wales.

From the statue go right and follow the
A482 out of town. Before you get to the
bridge over the Aeron ahead, turn into a
lane on the left called Bro Allt-y-Graig. Stay

on the lane until you pass a row of houses
on the right and go right onto a footpath
just after the last property in the row.

You are now on a cycle trail following
what was the old Lampeter-Aberaeron
branch railway, which closed in 1951.
It keeps close to the fast-flowing Aeron
– if you're lucky you may spot a kingfisher.

Stick with the trail for 2km until it arrives
at a minor road. Go left here to walk
towards the Llanerchaeron Estate, which is
run by the National Trust.

The mansion was designed by the
Georgian architect John Nash, who added
trademark touches to other estate
buildings: one is the Coachman's Cottage,
which you pass after leaving the cycle trail;
he also redesigned St Non's Church.

About 150m after St Non's, look out for a

◂ The harbour at Aberaeron

footpath signpost on the right just before the drive to the house. It points the way to a gap in the park wall and a public footpath that crosses the parkland.

To visit the house, carry on along the road for two or three minutes to the ticket office and café. There is also a riverside picnic area. You can use the first-class café without paying to go into the mansion, although a tour of the house is well worth the time.

Backtrack to the gap in the park wall and go through this to meet an iron gate. Cross the park, aiming for a wooden gate straight ahead at the midpoint between a large tree on the right and a clump of trees to the left. From the gate bear right towards trees on the far side of the field.

Here, cross the footbridge over the Afon Mydr and walk up to a track to turn left. You soon come to a path on the right and the mansion's old station halt nearby.

If you want to walk back to Aberaeron, take this path, which soon links up with the cycle trail. Alternatively, keep walking up the track to the A482 – you'll see the bus stop 100m away to the south.

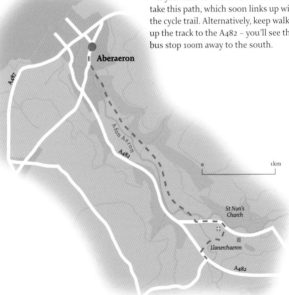

Aberaeron to Aberarth

Distance 6.5km **Time** 3 hours
Terrain roads, paths, beach walking
Map OS Explorer 198 **Access** bus (T5) from
Aberystwyth and Cardigan to Aberaeron

**Busy Aberaeron and its small neighbour,
Aberarth, share a maritime tradition. This
route explores the coast between the two
as well as diving into the green hills that
lie just inland.**

Start out from Aberaeron's landmark
Harbourmaster Hotel, a four-square
building that dominates Quay Parade. In
Victorian times it doubled as pub and
harbourmaster's office. From an upper
room the harbourmaster was able to look
out from one window to see his busy
little harbour and from another Cardigan
Bay. At quieter times he would also take a
turn behind the bar.

Leaving the hotel, take a moment to
climb the look-out tower nearby and take
in the view of the town's colourful
terraces and the hills beyond. Aberaeron
harbour was built in 1807, along with
homes for the workers of the local
landowner, Rev Thomas-Jones Gwynne; a
new town was then built during following
decades to an architect's plan.

Head east out of town on the
promenade and, where it ends, keep
walking along the beach, leaving this at
the Coast Path sign to walk along the top
of the low, crumbling cliffs.

At Aberarth, bear right when you reach
a bench to take a lane to the main

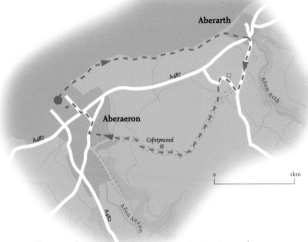

Aberarth

Aberaeron

A487

A487

Afon Arth

Cefntyncoed

A482

Afon Aeron

0 — 1km

Aberaeron-Aberystwyth
coast road. Go left and cross
the road to a country lane that meets the
main road at the river bridge. This lane
leads up out of the village – it's a steep
climb, so spare some time to enjoy views
over the Arth to the sea. At the first
junction, go right towards Llanddewi
Aberarth Church. Don't pass by without
taking a look around what has to be the
graveyard with the most spectacular views
in Wales.

Follow the lane down from the church
and around a bend to a stile on the left.
Go over this and take the path up the
slope to a gate. Another stile takes you
into the next field, where you bear right
to follow the line of the hedge to a third
stile. Climb over it and keep following the
track southwestwards until you reach a

gate out onto a tarmac lane.

Cross the lane to take the bridleway,
which heads westwards. In time the track
bears right, but keep to the signposted
bridleway that carries straight on instead.
This leads downhill to a country lane,
where you go right and, after about 250m,
leave the road to take a narrow footpath
on the right. This follows the line of a
small stream and skirts behind some
cottages. It also passes the town's leisure
centre before coming to a roundabout. Go
straight on at the roundabout and turn
right at the main road.

After 300m, turn left at the horse statue
onto Alban Square. Carry straight on to
Bridge Street and then go left before
crossing over into Market Street. At the
car park turn left and pass the Hive café to
return to Quay Parade.

◀ The Coast Path close to Aberarth

Llanon to Llanrhystud

Distance **5km (or 9.5km round trip)**
Time **2 hours (or 3 hours 45 round trip)**
Terrain **roads, green lanes and beach**
Map **OS Explorer 199** Access **buses (40, X50) from Aberystwyth and Cardigan stop in Llanon and Llanrhystud**

Llanrhystud and Llanon are two coastal community neighbours that share a backdrop of rolling green hills, which are a treat to explore.

Llanon is a busy little place with the main Cardigan-Aberystwyth road running through its heart. Start your walk at Stryd yr Ysgol, a side road near the village bus stop – there's a fish & chip shop on the junction. If you're arriving by car, there's a free car park on this road.

Walk up Stryd yr Ysgol to a junction and go left onto Heol Llain Prysg, a small side road. At the next junction keep right onto a bridleway, which soon climbs into the beautiful wooded Peris valley. Continue along this track, crossing a small wooden bridge and zigzagging up the steep valley side.

Bear right across a field to a metal gate, marked with a small bridleway disc. Go through this and up to a second field gate. At a barn go right and walk along the drive to a junction. Here, go left along a minor road, turning right at the next junction onto a lane, which passes the farm of Penfor-fawr.

Around 500m after the farm you come to a signposted bridleway on the left. This soon brings you to Allt Fawr, the high ground above Llanrhystud. Along the way you pass two Iron Age hillforts, Castell Mawr and Castell Bach. Although you are only about 120m above sea level at Castell Mawr, the drop to the coastal low land is

so steep that it feels far higher. The forts were built at a great vantage point.

Follow the bridleway as it drops down into Llanrhystud. In time it becomes a residential road called Glan yr Afon. At the main road turn right. The bus stop is close to the Black Horse pub further into the village.

Alternatively, you can walk back to Llanon using the beach (check tide times – it is best not attempted at high tide). At the end of Glan yr Afon, go left and then cross the road. Turn right onto a minor road opposite a petrol station and walk to the beach. From there head southwest.

As you get close to journey's end, you will see the tower of St Ffraed's Church ahead in the beachside hamlet of Llansantffraed – it is the parish church of both here and nearby Llanon.

A little further on the route crosses the Afon Peris where it flows

across the beach. Soon after, leave the beach on the path that runs alongside the Peris. At a bridge keep right. When you reach a fork in the road, go left into Stryd y Neuadd. This soon brings you back to Llanon. At the A487 go right and cross the road to get to Stryd yr Ysgol.

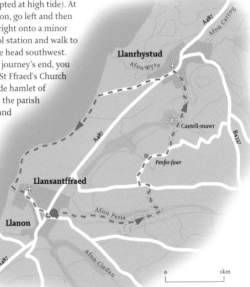

Approaching Aberystwyth from either the north or the south on the Ceredigion Coast Path, your first view of the town will be a bird's eye one. Aber sits between a pair of summits, Constitution Hill (Y Craig Glais) and Pen Dinas, both of which are excellent vantage points over this small town.

That it is small comes as a surprise to many, since Aberystwyth punches well above its weight. It is a place that serves many purposes. It has been a seaside resort since the 18th century and remains one of the liveliest in Wales. It is the shopping centre for a great swathe of Mid Wales and has lots of good cafés and restaurants. It is a nationally important cultural centre; the National Library of Wales is housed in an imposing building

overlooking the town and a number of important Welsh language organisations are based there too. And it is also a university town, which gives it something of a split personality. Aber has a year-round population of around 16,000, but in term time this is ramped up by up to 10,000 students.

Aber has two hills and it also has two rivers. Its name means 'Mouth of the Ystwyth', and the Ystwyth does flow to the sea just to the south of the town – but the river that flows through the heart of Aberystwyth is the Rheidol. It is a river in a hurry; its source in the Cambrian Mountains is less than 20 miles away and it is all whitewater and impatience as it races down to the sea.

The walks in this section explore Aberystwyth and the beautiful countryside that surrounds it, including walks in, and close to, the dramatic Rheidol and Ystwyth Valleys.

Aberystwyth and the Rheidol

Wild way to Llanrhystud

Distance 15km **Time** 5 hours (one way)
Terrain stony paths with some steep
sections **Map** OS Explorer 213
Access good bus and train services to
Aberystwyth; hourly bus (40) from
Llanrhystud back to the start

**This day walk along one of the wildest
stretches of the Ceredigion coast can be
an endurance test, but it is an exhilarating
experience that is well worth the effort.**

The best way to explore the coast south
of Aberystwyth is to walk the Coast Path
and catch a bus home. From the centre of
town cross the Afon Rheidol and then
walk along the main A487 road until you
pass the fire station.

Here, turn right into Pen-yr-Angor and
carry on to a bridge over the Afon
Ystwyth. Crossing the bridge brings you
to the end of the harbour breakwater.

Now walk south at the top of
Tanybwlch Beach. At the end of this beach
the Coast Path climbs sharply, gaining
more than 100m in height in less than
500m distance.

In time you will see the caravan site at
Morfa Bychan ahead. Here, the path drops
down towards the caravans and brings
you to a kissing gate which opens into a
field above the site.

Bear left and head uphill until you see a
fingerpost, which you now aim for. The
path takes you on to a second kissing gate

by a stream, opening onto a lane. Turn left to walk along the lane for 30m and then take the footpath on the right.

Climb the slope ahead to a waymark post and follow the path until it brings you to a road, where you should go right. Just a few paces on, turn right again onto a track marked 'Llety r Gegin'.

Stay on the track towards the clifftops and follow the Coast Path waymarking south towards the derelict farm at Ffos Las. Pass to the left of the farmhouse and take the track on the left uphill.

At a fingerpost bear right. The next section of the route keeps close to the eroding cliffs, taking you to another farm, Mynachdy'r-graig. As you approach the farm go left to a kissing gate, which opens onto a footbridge. Cross the bridge and cross the farmyard on a track that takes you on to a long uphill stretch of path.

For the next 4km the path keeps close to the sea and is well signposted. Along the way you pass above woods at Penderi, where oaks clinging to the face of the steep cliffs are a nesting site for ravens, buzzards and kestrels.

In time, where the path drops down towards the beach, bear left to a footbridge and stile. Cross the stile and go right, heading across the field to a kissing gate in the next fence.

Go left from here to reach a fingerpost, where you turn right to follow the field boundary above

a caravan site. At the driveway to the site, go left and then follow the lane to the A487. Turn left here for a short walk to the bus stop, outside the Black Lion pub.

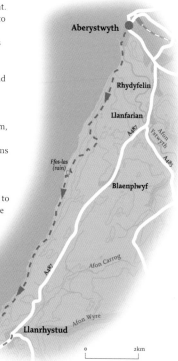

Aberystwyth town circular

Distance **3km** Time **1 hour**
Terrain **town roads; steep climb near start**
Map **OS Explorer 213** Access **good bus and
train services to Aberystwyth**

**Aberystwyth is a fascinating town. It is
not a big place, but is Wales' liveliest
seaside resort as well as being an
important cultural centre.**

For most visitors, Aberystwyth's main
attraction is that it is a seaside town. It
has three beaches, but the best-known is
North Beach, with its promenade and
pier. Start your tour overlooking North
Beach at the junction of Terrace Road and
Marine Terrace.

Victorian visitors believed sea-bathing
was good for them and an 1870s'
pamphlet sold the town to prospective

visitors on the basis that though
accessible from all of Britain, it was 'still
placed at such a distance from the larger
manufacturing towns as to secure for it
almost a complete immunity from the
visits of a certain class of daily
excursionist...'

Head north along the Prom towards
Constitution Hill. At the end of the Prom,
go right to the red brick Aberystwyth Cliff
Railway building. The railway was opened
in 1896 and is Britain's longest electric
cliff railway. It gets its passengers to the
hilltop at a stately 4mph.

Turn right onto Queen's Road, passing
the old Town Hall before crossing the
junction where Queen's Road ends to
carry on along Thespian Street.

Go right into Alexandra Road towards

the railway station. This is the terminus both for mainline services and the narrow-gauge Vale of Rheidol Railway. Cross Alexandra Road at the front of the station and head up Terrace Road before turning left onto Great Darkgate Street. The name of Aberystwyth's main shopping street is an echo of the town's medieval past – an entryway through the early town wall was called Dark Gate.

At the end of Great Darkgate Street follow the road round to the left and then go right along Sea View Place. Enter the castle grounds – a good place for a picnic, with a children's playground and a crazy golf course – and walk towards the promenade.

Aberystwyth's castle has seen eventful times. Built in the 13th century, when the Norman rulers of England were struggling to control areas of Wales taken from native princes, the castle replaced an earlier fortress just south of the town that was destroyed by the Welsh. Aberystwyth Castle has been besieged twice, once in the 1400s when it was held by the army of Owain Glyndwr, the self-proclaimed Prince of Wales, and again in the 1600s during the Civil War.

From the castle walk along the New Promenade heading northwards. The large building that fronts onto it is the Old College,

which was originally intended to be a hotel, but became Aberystwyth's university.

At the pier, turn right along Pier Street and then left onto Eastgate. At the end of Eastgate turn left to return to your start point on Marine Terrace.

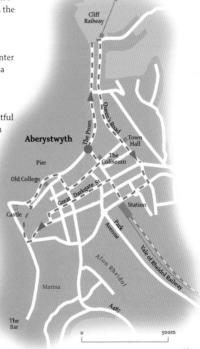

◀ The Old College on Aberystwyth Prom

49

Pen Dinas and the Wellington Monument

Distance **3.5km** Time **1 hour 15**
Terrain **stony paths, roads**
Map **OS Explorer 213** Access **good bus and train services to Aberystwyth**

Pen Dinas is a hill with warrior connections. Its summit is ringed by an Iron Age hillfort and, more recently, it was chosen as the location for a monument in memory of Napoleon Bonaparte's nemesis, the Duke of Wellington.

The Trefechan Bridge at the bottom of Bridge Street is the start point for this trip south of the Rheidol. Cross the bridge into Trefechan and follow the A487 as it begins to climb out of town.

Look for a footpath sign on the right opposite Aberystwyth Holiday Village. A narrow path climbs the hillside and soon enters the nature reserve, which takes in the hill's summit.

In time there are great views over Aberystwyth and you get your first glimpse of the Wellington Monument on the hilltop ahead. Built in 1852, the original plan was to top it with a statue of Wellington on horseback but that turned out to be too expensive.

At the gate go right onto a farm track for 200m or so and then pass through two kissing gates. Soon after the second gate the path swings to the left to enter Pen Dinas hillfort.

After heading along the ridge to the monument, take the stony path southeastwards, which soon zigzags down the hillside. In time you'll see houses ahead and the path brings you to a gate at the reserve boundary where three paths meet.

Don't go through the gate; instead, pass it and drop downhill (ignoring the path on your right) through gorse and hawthorn scrub. As you get closer to the River Ystwyth go left onto a grassy area, where there's a round shelter.

Pass to the right of the roundhouse to a gate that opens onto a cycle trail. Go right along the trail, which in time becomes a minor road. Follow the lane until you reach the first bungalows on the right. Opposite the third of these is a small footpath, which takes you between gardens to a road.

Unless you're in a hurry it's worth detouring left at this point and crossing the bridge over the river to explore the beach and the harbour's outer wall. The harbour offers boats a safe refuge when stormy weather hits Cardigan Bay, but in the days of sail getting to safety took skill and luck. For example, the men aboard the *John and Mary* learned a hard lesson in February 1847 when they failed to manoeuvre their vessel into the harbour entrance.

The ship was driven onto its side on the beach a stone's throw from safety. The crew had to take to the ship's rigging to save themselves, and hundreds of townspeople gathered to watch the rescue attempt – two men were saved, but two unlucky sailors were lost.

From the beach retrace your steps across the bridge and along the minor road towards the harbour. Look out for a Ceredigion Coast Path sign that directs you to the left – the path keeps close to the edge of the wall around the southern side of the harbour to return you to Trefechan Bridge.

◄ Approaching the Wellington Monument on Pen Dinas

Constitution Hill

Distance 5.5km Time 2 hours
Terrain good path and minor roads
Map OS Explorer 213 Access good bus and
train services to Aberystwyth; take the
cliff railway if you prefer to miss the climb

The massive presence of Constitution Hill
seems to loom over the northern end of
Aberystwyth's seafront Promenade. This
route takes you to the 130m summit for
breathtaking views and through beautiful
woodland too.

Starting out from the northern end of
the Promenade, aim for the redbrick Cliff
Railway building and take the path on the
left, signposted Coast Path. This zigzags up
the hillside and in time crosses a bridge
over the railway track.

On the far side keep left up a flight of
steps to cross back over a second bridge.

Then climb uphill along the line of the cliff
edge to a Coast Path fingerpost.

From the fingerpost the path bears
northwards and in time drops down
towards the bay at Clarach. Where it comes
to a road, go right until you come to a
postbox where you take the path which
rises into the woodland opposite.

Stay on this path to a waymarked gate
and then pass a house to carry straight on
along a minor road. In spring these woods
are filled with the ice-white flowers and
heady scent of wild garlic.

At the end of the road, continue straight
on along a waymarked bridleway into
woodland. Just after the old quarry bear
right at the fork in the path. When the
bridleway reaches a road (the B4572) go
right to take a footpath that rises back up
into the woods and away from the road.

◀ The Cliff Railway track
on Constitution Hill

After 250m, where the path
comes to a crossroads of routes,
go straight on to a stile.

Climb over the stile and carry straight
on to a gate on the horizon. Go through
this and over another stile a few steps on.
At the fingerpost head straight on,
following the fenceline towards two ruined
farm buildings. Between the two ruins is a
stile to a track.

Take the track downhill, passing a
turning on the left, to reach a kissing gate
on the left. This opens onto a path into a
wood and then along the edge of a golf
course. Stay on this path by a stone wall all
the way into Parc Penglais, a nature
reserve. Where the wall ends, four paths
dive into the woods – take the one that's

second from the left. This leads downhill
to a high wooden fence where you bear
right (do not go down the flight of steps)
to carry on into the wood, passing an owl
sculpture along the way.

The path heads down towards the town,
eventually passing the backs of houses to
bring you to the junction of North Road
and Infirmary Road. Follow North Road
northwards, turn left into Queen's Avenue
at the end and then right onto Queen's
Road. At the end of Queen's Road you
come to the cliff railway and, to your left,
the north end of the Prom.

Rheidol Falls

Distance **4km** Time **1 hour 15**
Terrain **minor roads, tracks and footpaths**
Map OS Explorer 213 Access **bus (525) from
Aberystwyth stops at nearby Goginan**

**Get away from it all with this easy-going
stroll around Cwm Rheidol Reservoir. It is
a great family walk – kids will love
crossing the footbridge high above the
river just below thundering Rheidol Falls.**

Cwm Rheidol is a beautiful place to
while away a day, which makes it hard to
square with the fact that it is also at the
centre of the largest hydropower scheme in
England and Wales. Altogether the system
of reservoirs, dams and aqueducts covers
an area of more than 160 sq km and
generates enough electricity to supply
more than 12,000 homes.

The start point for this walk is the car
park at the plant's visitor centre. Open to
the public at Easter and during summer
(May to end of September), the centre has
a free educational exhibit about renewable
energy for the children and a café. You can
join guided tours of the power station
itself, further along the valley.

As you leave the car park go left and walk
along the road that runs around the
reservoir. In time you pass a phonebox,
where there are great views along the
valley to the east towards the hills around
Devil's Bridge.

Continue along the road as it drops
down towards the power station. When
you come to a house on the left called
Rheidol View, turn down the footpath
opposite, which soon brings you to a metal

◂ Rheidol Falls

footbridge over the Afon Rheidol.

The bridge offers great views of the falls a little further upriver, as does the picnic area on the far bank – pass the gate to this to reach a stile on the right.

After climbing over the stile, take the path uphill through bushes to a track. Keep left here and pass a ruined cottage to walk along a fenceline.

As you walk don't be surprised if you hear the whistle of an approaching steam engine; the Vale of Rheidol Railway runs along the valley a little above where you're walking. When you come to a gate across the track use the stile alongside it and then head straight on through the woods.

You soon come to a junction with another path. Go right and then straight on at the next path junction. On this stretch of the route, look out for bare patches of hillside among the trees on the far side of the valley. These are the spoil heaps left by mines that operated during the second half of the 19th century.

The route continues through the lakeside woods, passing the dam and eventually arriving at a minor road. Here, go right to walk towards the river.

The road crosses a bridge above a weir across the Rheidol before coming to a road junction. Turn right to walk alongside the reservoir back to the visitor centre, a distance of about 400m.

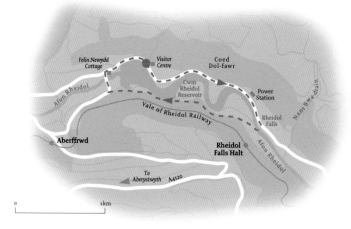

Kites of Nant yr Arian

Distance **1km** Time **30 minutes**
Terrain **all-ability path with a few gentle
gradients** Map OS Explorer 213
Access bus (525) from Aberystwyth to
Llanidloes stops on request

**Once one of Britain's rarest birds of prey,
the red kite is now a relatively common
sight throughout Ceredigion. But for a
guaranteed kite encounter head for the
afternoon 'show' at the forest visitor
centre at Bwlch Nant yr Arian.**

On the western edge of the Cambrian
Mountains, the Bwlch Nant yr Arian
Visitor Centre is about 16km as the kite
flies from the coast of Cardigan Bay.
But on a clear day you can see all the way
to the twin hills that frame Aberystwyth.

The centre is part of a working forest
that was until recently run by the Forestry
Commission, but is now part of National
Resources Wales. There are a number of
forest walks from the centre and the

shortest of them, the Barcud Trail, is
an all-ability route that has been laid out
to be as wheelchair and buggy-friendly
as possible.

It is a pleasant walk around the centre's
lake through mature conifer woods and
there are good views of the hills to the
north and east, but what makes it a must-
do for any visitor to Ceredigion is the
daily ritual of kite-feeding.

Kites were once a common sight even
in towns and cities, where they scavenged
in the streets. But from the 1500s
onwards they were seen as a nuisance
and persecuted, causing numbers to
drop sharply.

By the middle of the 20th century they
were extinct in England and Scotland.
However, in Wales just a handful of
breeding pairs survived in the wilds of the
central mountains. In the last couple of
decades, their fortunes have changed and
now there are thought to be more than

◄ A red kite soars over Bwlch Nant yr Arian

1000 breeding pairs throughout Wales. The comeback has been supported through the efforts of bird lovers who have set up feeding stations where meat scraps are put out for kites. One of the most successful of these is Bwlch Nant yr Arian. The centre's team have been feeding 'their' kites ever since 1999 and on winter days the birds turn up to eat in their hundreds.

Food is put out each day, including on Christmas Day – at 2pm during the winter and at 3pm in summer. Kites fly in from up to 16km for a share of the hand-out and they are often joined by other meat-eating species, like ravens and buzzards.

From the car park, take the path on the left to head down to the lakeside trail to walk anti-clockwise around the lake. If you are arriving shortly before feeding time you will see birds heading towards the centre from all directions.

There are benches at the side of the path that are perfectly placed to watch the kites fly in. They don't like to land unless it is absolutely necessary, which makes for impressive aerial acrobatics.

When feeding is over complete your circuit of the lake to visit the centre, which has a nice café with views to the lake and hills.

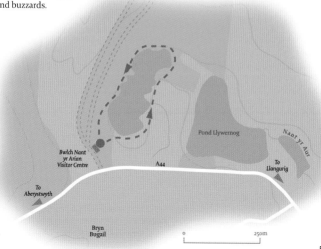

Pond Llywernog

Nant yr Aur

Bwlch Nant
yr Arian
Visitor Centre

A44

To
Llangurig

To
Aberystwyth

Bryn
Bugail

0   250m

Devil's Bridge

Distance 1.25km **Time** 45 minutes
Terrain good paths, but lots of steps
Map OS Explorer 198 **Access** train or bus
(YP22) from Aberystwyth to Devil's Bridge

Devil's Bridge was probably Ceredigion's first tourist location. Visitors have been making the journey to witness its natural splendour since the 18th century and on this walk you'll discover why.

Two fast-flowing upland rivers – the Mynach and the Rheidol – meet at Devil's Bridge in a dramatic steep-sided gorge that is wild and beautiful. It is an amazing place, especially in summer when the gorge has a rainforest feel to it.

Start your walk at the Aberystwyth-Devil's Bridge railway terminus. The narrow gauge Vale of Rheidol Railway was built in the 1890s to serve local mines and to carry visitors up from the coast.

Getting here on the train is a joy, but if you're travelling by car, time your arrival to be at the station just before a train's departure. That way you can see one of the railway's locomotives.

From the station, go left to walk to the roadbridge. Cross over and make for the entrance of the gorge path, which is on the left. You do have to pay to enter the gorge walk.

After passing through the turnstile, head down a flight of steps and then go left to a viewpoint just below the gorge's bridges. The legend goes that it was beyond mere mortals to bridge the Mynach. The Devil agreed to build one in return for the soul of the first living being to cross, but when it was completed the Devil was outsmarted. An old woman threw a scrap of bread across and her dog scampered over ahead of her.

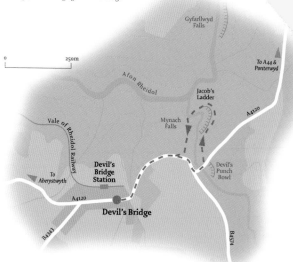

◀ Descending into the river gorge at Devil's Bridge

Gyfarllwyd
Falls

To A44 &
Ponterwyd

A4120

Jacob's
Ladder

Mynach
Falls

Afon Rheidol

Vale of Rheidol Railway

Devil's
Punch
Bowl

Devil's
Bridge
Station

To
Aberystwyth

A4120

Devil's Bridge

B4343

B4574

0   250m

The first – and lowest – of the three bridges is thought to have been built in the 12th century. The middle one dates from the 18th century and it was replaced in 1901 with the iron bridge that is still in use today.

Backtrack to the path and drop downhill to the second viewpoint with fine views along the valley to the summit of Bryn y Castell to the west. If you're lucky you may see a train crossing the hillside.

The path works its way down into the gorge and as you walk the roar of the Mynach Falls gets louder. In time you come to a gazebo, situated to frame views of the series of falls that takes the Mynach to its confluence with the Rheidol.

Continue along the path to go down a steep flight of steps known as Jacob's Ladder and then cross a footbridge before zigzagging back up the side of the gorge. Look out for a short path on the left that takes you to a grotto next to the falls. It is said that it was once a robbers' hideout.

Retrace your steps to the path and carry on up the side of the gorge. When you reach the road go right back to the station.

DEVIL'S BRIDGE

Hafod and the Ystwyth Gorge

Distance **3.6km** Time **1 hour 30**
Terrain **forest tracks and paths**
Map **OS Explorer 213** Access **a community
bus (T22) serves nearby Cwmystwyth**

**The Hafod Estate is unique. Its grand
house is long gone, but much of the
striking landscaped estate that it once
occupied remains and is a joy to explore.**

Once owned by the monks of Strata
Florida Abbey, Hafod later came into the
hands of a wealthy local family. Over the
years their estate was improved, but the
most striking changes happened in the
late 18th century when it was owned by
Thomas Johnes.

An enthusiast for the contemporary
fashion of all things 'Picturesque', he

carried out landscaping that he hoped
would accentuate the Ystwyth Valley's
wild beauty. His project made Hafod
famous and attracted leading artists and
writers. Sadly, the estate's fortunes
changed – by the mid-20th century the
mansion stood abandoned and it was
demolished in the late 1950s.

Now it is managed by a charity, the
Hafod Trust, paths have been restored
and there are colour-coded walking routes
through the estate.

This walk combines sections of three of
them. From the car park and picnic area
follow the signs for the blue trail past
Hafod Church. Keep left and stay on the
blue route, which zigzags downhill.

When you come to a track, cross straight

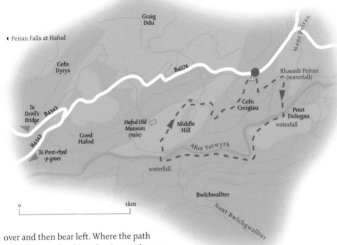

◄ Peiran Falls at Hafod

over and then bear left. Where the path splits it is worth taking the time to detour (right) a short way to see Peiran Falls, an attractive little waterfall.

From the waterfall backtrack to where the path splits and go right to follow a path marked with green arrows. Cross a footbridge and head straight on through the woods.

Where the path comes close to the edge of the woodland, go right on the green trail. This soon brings you to one of the walk's highlights, a chainbridge over the river gorge.

Cross the bridge and bear right to walk above the river to another footbridge. After crossing the water walk to a gate, going through this and across a track to take a path between trees.

At a stile go right to walk along the edge of a field to a second stile. Climb over the

stile to a track where you go left.

At a Y-junction go right and then stay on the track to a signpost that points the way into the woods. In time you will come to another of the estate's landmarks, the Rustic Bridge.

From here, walk on through conifers to another footbridge and go right to join another track at a waymark post.

Go straight on across the grass to a parallel track and then left. At the next waymark post, go right to follow the blue trail and keep right to climb the hillside and pass a cottage. Go over the stile and then bear left to cross the next field to first one stile and then a second.

At a waymark post go left to follow the blue trail uphill back to the car park.

There is more to Ceredigion than its coast, and the Afon Teifi is central to its identity as a county. For part of its course it forms the boundary with neighbouring Carmarthenshire, and from its source in the moorland above Strata Florida to the point that it flows into Cardigan Bay, it runs for 120km, making it the longest river to complete its source to sea journey within the borders of Wales.

The walks in this chapter have been selected to highlight the best of the Teifi as it changes mood and tempo and the varied and delightful landscapes that it travels through. While at Strata Florida it is a young, fast-running whitewater river just a couple of strides wide, at Lampeter it is characterised by snaky meanders across a wide, flat valley, and at Cenarth it becomes a dramatic series of roaring, churning falls.

Some of the best farming country in Wales can be found in the Teifi Valley. And there are plenty of opportunities to test the reputation of locally-produced lamb and Welsh Black beef, artisan-produced cheeses and the traditional cawl, a meat and vegetable soup, for yourself.

Strung along the banks of the Teifi are a series of towns that owe their development to their situation at crossing points over the river. Walks in this chapter explore Lampeter and Newcastle Emlyn, both great examples of the Welsh market town.

Along the Teifi

A485

8

7

Tregaron

ampeter

6

Cenarth Falls

Distance 2km **Time** 30 minutes
Terrain uneven and muddy in places
Map OS Explorer 185 **Access** bus (460) from
Cardigan and Newcastle Emlyn to Cenarth

**The dramatic falls at Cenarth have
attracted visitors for centuries. Spend
some time watching the churning
whitewater before exploring the Teifi's
banks, perfect for an afternoon stroll. Part
of this route follows a riverside path that
can flood, so it is best not attempted
when the river is high.**

Park considerately at the roadside in the
village or use the free public car park,
which is about 200m from the post office
on the B4332 to Boncath.

Start at the old bridge over the Teifi,
which was built in the 1780s and remains
an important river crossing. The view
from here is impressive all year round, but
in winter the river is wild. When the Teifi
is in full spate you can hear the roar of the
water throughout the village. The source
of the Teifi in the Cambrian Mountains is
around 160km from Cenarth and during
wet weather water cascades off the steep
slopes and soon transforms the river into
a raging force.

From the car park next to the bridge,
pass the small stone cottage and take the
riverside path bearing east past the
viewing platform, a good place to watch
for jumping salmon in September and

◄ The old mill and falls at Cenarth

October or sewin (sea trout) in July and August.

When the traveller Gerald of Wales visited Cenarth in the 1180s he was impressed by the leaping salmon that he saw. The fish were able to leap up the falls 'about as far as the height of the tallest spear', he noted.

The building on the far bank of the river is the village's old watermill, the successor of earlier mills that date back to at least the 1200s. The current building remained in use until the 1960s and is now part of the National Coracle Centre.

Traditional coracles, or small rounded boats, are made using a willow and hazel frame. They are now used only on the Teifi and two other Welsh rivers.

Follow the path into the steep-sided, wooded valley. The falls are soon out of earshot and the tea-brown, peaty Teifi flows quietly below arching tree boughs. In time the path turns away from the riverbank to climb steeply through woods, which in spring are carpeted with bluebells. At the minor road, go left.

The road runs between a tall hedge on the right and, on the left, a near-vertical drop down to the river. It is thickly wooded, but when the trees are not in leaf you can glimpse the water beneath you.

Drop down to the village, turning left opposite the village Methodist Chapel to return to the bridge.

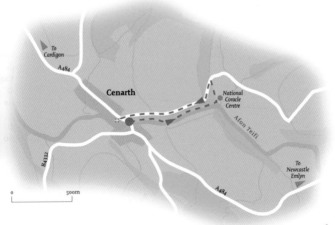

Newcastle Emlyn and the Dragon's castle

Distance 1km **Time** 30 minutes
Terrain pavements and park paths
Map OS Explorer 198 **Access** bus (460) from
Cardigan to Newcastle Emlyn

Adpar and Emlyn were separate
communities at a time when Emlyn's
castle was still new – close to eight
centuries ago. They later became a single
borough, which today is the archetypal
Welsh market town.

Newcastle Emlyn is a great place for a
picnic on a sunny day. First pick up some
good things to eat from the town's busy
main street and then head for the ruins of
the castle that gives the town its name.

When King Henry III gave the lands
along the west bank of the River Teifi to a
Welsh lord in the 13th century, that lord –

Meredith ap Rhys Gryg – felt he needed
a castle to feel secure. The site he chose
on a small hill in a great arcing loop of
the Teifi was perfect from a military point
of view.

Now a park with the castle ruins at its
centre, the all-round views that Meredith
saw as a defensive advantage are now an
attraction for locals and visitors.

If driving to the start, park considerately
at the roadside on Lloyds Terrace (B4333) in
Adpar, then walk to the junction with the
B4571. Turn right and walk down to the
imposing stone roadbridge over the Teifi.
It is quite narrow, so use the footbridge to
the right. As you cross the Teifi you leave
Ceredigion and venture for a time into
neighbouring Carmarthenshire.

Head up Bridge Street until you reach

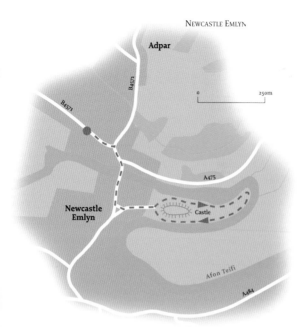

Adpar

B4571

B4571

A475

Newcastle Emlyn

Castle

0   250m

Afon Teifi

A484

the old Market Hall with its clocktower. Walk left into Castle Street, the small road behind the Market Hall. Go straight on along Castle Street to a gate topped by a wrought iron dragon.

The dragon is a reference to a local legend that the town and surrounding countryside was once terrorised by a giant reptile, either a large viper or a wyvern – a winged dragon. It turned up one market day and settled down to sleep on the castle walls. A brave soldier is said to have woken the monster up and tricked it into swooping down on a red cloak that he had spread out on the river. As it died it polluted the water with black venom.

One theory is that the dragon story may have links with the time when forces of the rebel leader Owain Glyndwr captured the castle in 1403 and held it for a few weeks before they fled from a large English army. While they held the castle, the rebels flew a dragon banner.

After soaking up the atmosphere and views, take the concrete path that passes to the left of the ruins. It soon brings you to the banks of the Teifi.

Follow the riverbank path around the loop of the meander. In time the path passes the castle again and then climbs back to the park entrance – from here, retrace your steps to Adpar.

◀ The ruins of Emlyn's castle

...he Teifi

...nor roads
...(460) from
...yn to Henllan

Broad and slow-flowing upstream, the Teifi undergoes something of a personality change at Henllan. On this walk you see both faces of the river – easy-going and whitewater.

Whether you're arriving by car or bus, the start point for this walk is Henllan's railway station. Passenger services ended in the early 1950s, but since 1983 part of the line has been run by steam enthusiasts as the Teifi Valley Railway.

From the entrance of the station walk north along the B4334, ignoring a turning on the left to continue before branching right onto a track as you approach a house on the right.

At Parc, an abandoned farm, bear right to cross a stile into a field and then left to pass a huge oak – before coming to a waymark post, which indicates a path into woodland. Stay on this path until it reaches a second waymark post, where you go left. The route leads to a gate opening onto a bridge. Cross the bridge and walk through the woods to go left at another waymark post.

When you reach a stile, climb over it to

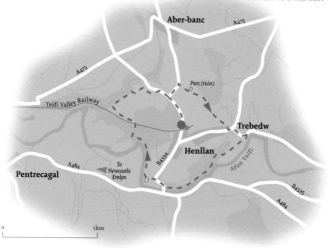

Aber-banc
A475

A475

Parc (ruin)

Teifi Valley Railway

Trebedw

Henllan

Afon Teifi

A484
To
Newcastle
Emlyn

B4334

Pentrecagal

B4335

A484

0   1km

walk down to one gate and then on to a second, passing a house on your left. Within a few paces you arrive at a road.

Go left here, cross a bridge and turn right at the first road junction. Walk past a large house and look out for a footpath sign on the right, which points the way towards the Teifi.

Cross the meadow to a kissing gate on the far side, then bear right to go over a footbridge. The path bears left to the banks of the Teifi. Follow the river to Henllan Bridge and then walk up to the B4334 and turn right. At the first bend take the signposted footpath on the left, which passes the parish church.

At a gate, cross the stile, passing the waterworks to reach a second stile leading from one field to another. Here, carry straight on to the woods on the far side,

where a path brings you to a footbridge.

Beyond this, the path follows the course of the river, but when this swings away to the left keep straight on to cross a stile and go left at the track.

Look for a stile on the right which you cross to join a path into woods. After about 70m, a small stream crosses the trail which shortly splits into three.

Take the path on the right, which leads through the woods for another 75m or so to pass under the railway. Stay on the track until it nears a gate and yard ahead; just before the gate, go right to first one stile and then a second.

Follow the hedgeline down to a third stile in the corner of the field and then right onto a track. At the road go right to a road junction, where you go right again to return to the station.

◂ An oak tree near Parc Farm, Henllan

Coed y Foel woodland stroll

Distance 6km **Time** 2 hours
Terrain woodland and farm paths, country
lanes **Map** OS Explorer 185 **Access** bus
(621) from Pencader to nearby Llandysul
via Ffostrasol

The attractive little riverside town of
Llandysul was once a centre of industry –
water-driven woollen mills manufactured
fine Welsh woollens. It is a place with a
laid-back feel, and the surrounding hills
make for great walking.

One of the best walks takes you through
Coed y Foel, a woodland nature reserve
that you can see from the town's High
Street on a clear day. In spring it is awash
with bluebells and in autumn a feast of
colour too.

The start point for this circuit is the
Woodland Trust car park. Go through the
gate into the trees and along a path by the
side of the fast-flowing Afon Gwernffrwd.

Cross the stream at the footbridge and
then take the path up into the woodland. It
follows the line of the Gwernffrwd on a
gentle climb.

The trees on this steep-sided valley are
mainly sessile oaks. The land was clear-
felled to provide timber during the First
World War, so the wood represents a
century's worth of growth. It is a great
place to look out for birds such as the
redstart and wood warbler, and in autumn
you can see jays collecting acorns.

When you come to a bench the path
bears right and runs alongside a tree-lined
bank to a marker post. This directs you to
the right and down a flight of steps.

By the veteran ash tree, go right to leave
the wood. Then cross the stream to climb
steps to a gate onto a forest track.

Go right and ignore the left fork that you

◀ A path climbs into Coed y Foel nature reserve

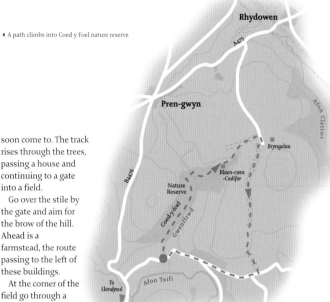

soon come to. The track rises through the trees, passing a house and continuing to a gate into a field.

Go over the stile by the gate and aim for the brow of the hill. Ahead is a farmstead, the route passing to the left of these buildings.

At the corner of the field go through a gate, ignoring a stile on your right to cross a second stile into another field. Follow the line of the hedge until you arrive at a lane, turning right here to pass around a smallholding on your right.

Where the tarmac ends at a gate, keep left to take the bridleway (rather than the footpath) and follow it along a beech tree avenue, continuing until you come to a field gate. Go through this and keep bearing south with the hedge on your right.

At a pair of gates, go through the left-hand gate onto a track. Later, at a fork by a waymark post, go right to a gate and then head diagonally across the next field to a second gate in its right-hand corner.

This leads into yet another field where you follow the line of the hedge a short way downhill to a final field gate opening onto a track. This soon brings you to a minor road where you turn right.

Follow this road for just over 1km, passing a farm on the way back to the reserve car park.

Peterwell and the Teifi meadows

Distance 3km **Time** 40 minutes
Terrain footpaths and town roads
Map OS Explorer 199 **Access** bus (40) from
Aberystwyth to Lampeter

**This circular walk around Lampeter is
perfect for a summer's day, taking you
along flower-rich meadows close to the
banks of the Teifi.**

Start on the High Street at the imposing
Town Hall, which was built in the 1820s as
a courthouse. Its moment in history came
in the 1940s when a soldier called William
Killick stood in the dock accused of an
attempt on the life of the poet Dylan
Thomas. Killick had taken exception to
Dylan Thomas' friendship with his wife
and shot at the poet, but he was acquitted

at Lampeter. The story inspired the 2008
film *The Edge of Love*, which was partly
filmed on location in the town.

From the Town Hall, head west on the
A475 until the road crosses a stream. Here,
look for a footpath on the left which
drops down steps and then follows the
stream to a gap in a hedge.

After the hedge the route joins a track
that takes you towards the Teifi. The
bumpy field you pass through was once
the site of an imposing mansion and is
notorious for ghostly goings on.

The house, Peterwell, was the home of
Lampeter's bad baronet, Sir Herbert Lloyd,
who was Lord of Lampeter in the 1750s.
Described by one of his enemies as 'a
scoundrelly dog', he cheated and

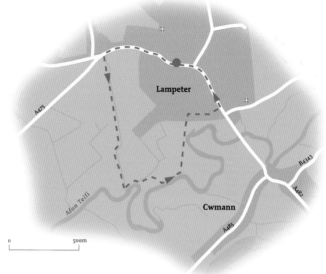

threatened his neighbours at every opportunity – and as a Justice of the Peace he was able to bring anyone who crossed him to court and then punish them for their 'crimes'.

After his death his home was left to fall into disrepair and the stone was carted away. Now it is said that the meadows around Peterwell are haunted – by the baronet himself or, possibly, by the tormented spirit of one of his victims.

After Peterwell, the path follows the stream until it reaches a footbridge by the Teifi. From the bridge, aim for the river, then straight on along the edge of the field to a second footbridge on the right.

Go over the bridge and then cross a field to a white-topped post close to the river.

At the post go left to follow the riverbank to a stile. Cross another field, aiming for a gap in the far hedge, and then head towards the far corner of the next field.

After crossing a stile here, aim for the houses that you can see ahead. The path passes between the gardens of two houses to bring you to a cul-de-sac.

Turn right and, at the first junction you come to, go right again into New Street. At the end of New Street, turn left onto Bridge Street, which is the main road through the town.

When you get to a mini-roundabout, head straight on to join the High Street, where it is just a short walk back to the Town Hall.

◀ A heron flies low over the Teifi at Lampeter

73

Long Wood over Lampeter

Distance 6km **Time 2 hours**
Terrain **woodland paths and tracks,
bridleways** Map **OS Explorer 199**
Access **bus (40) from Aberystwyth
to Lampeter**

**Lampeter is set in a beautiful landscape of
woods and rolling hills. It is just a short
walk from the university campus up into
Long Wood, an ancient woodland that pre-
dates the town itself.**

Although hardly bigger than a village,
Lampeter has had a university since 1822.
Now part of Trinity Saint David's, it is the
third oldest degree-awarding institution in
England and Wales – only Oxford and
Cambridge pre-date it. The university was
built on the castle site, which was donated
by a local landowner.

This walk starts from the gate of the
main university building in College Street.
From here, head out of town on North
Road and then take the road on the right
just after the rugby ground. Cross the Afon
Dulas and aim for the farm on the hillside,
which is called Mount Pleasant Farm.

When you reach the first of the farm
buildings, go left across a field to a small
metal gate in the corner. Go through the
gate and follow the edge of the wood until
you reach a gate.

Pass through the gate and follow the
green lane through the beech wood to a
second gate, a fingerpost and a smaller
gate on the left. Go through the smaller
gate and bear left onto the bridleway into
woodland.

Long Wood is owned and run by a

◀ The beech avenue near Lampeter's Mount Pleasant Farm

community co-operative, which took it over in 2003. It produces timber, but is also managed for recreation – look out for wood sculptures, a roundhouse and an atmospheric open air theatre.

The bridleway takes you to a gate and on to a second gate back into woods. At a signpost go right towards Hob's Garden; a short walk uphill brings you to the theatre, sculptures and garden.

From the theatre, backtrack to a fork in the path and go right (SP 'Castell Goetre'). Follow the path until the trees thin and you reach a fork, where you go right to reach a stile.

Crossing the stile takes you out of the wood and marks the beginning of the return journey to Lampeter. Bear right to follow a bridleway along the edge of the wood. The hillock ahead is actually the embankment of Allt-goch hillfort, one of two Iron Age enclosures along the ridge. Centuries of erosion have taken their toll on the fort, but it is still a great vantage point. To the north is Derry Ormond Tower, which was built in the 1830s to create employment for local men.

Go around the hillfort on its right and follow the field boundary, a line of big old beech trees. Dropping downhill you eventually come to a gate, which you should go through to carry on downhill on a bridleway.

Stay on this bridleway through a series of fields with the wood on your right. In time you arrive back at the point where you entered the community wood; retrace your steps to Lampeter.

Map labels:
Long Wood
Castell Allt-goch
Olwen Wood
Blaen-Plwyf-Isaf
A485
Afon Dulas
A482
Upper Forest
Mount Pleasant Farm
Lampeter
Lampeter University
A475
Afon Teifi
B4343
Cwmann
A482
Treherbert

0   1km

Cors Caron Nature Reserve

Distance **4km** Time **1 hour**
Terrain **good paths and boardwalk**
Map OS Explorer 199 Access **bus (T21) from Aberystwyth to Pontrhydfendigaid**

Cors Caron is one of Wales' wild places, an expanse of wetland that has been 12,000 years in the making. Now protected as a National Nature Reserve, it is a fascinating place that has a strange bleak beauty.

What makes Cors Caron such an important wetland is down to moss and lots of water. Sphagnum bogmoss has flourished over centuries, slowly filling what was once a huge lake in the broad Teifi Valley. Over time dead moss has formed layers of peat to create what is called a raised mire – the moss forms huge pillowy domes that are up to 5m high.

It is a good place to go wildlife-watching at any time of year, but is probably at its best in early summer. Then it is covered with swaying, white cottongrass and scores of dragonflies and electric-blue damselflies flit around peat-black pools.

In all, the nature reserve is 6km from end to end and most of it isn't open to visitors, but for an accessible 'taste' of the place there is a 1.5km boardwalk. This takes you out into the wetland – but means your feet stay dry.

The start point for this boardwalk excursion is the reserve's visitor car park, which is 3km north of Tregaron on the B4343. There is a bus service from Tregaron, but buses are infrequent. An alternative is to walk from Tregaron along the Ystwyth Trail, a cyclepath that partly runs along what was once the Great Western Railway line between Manchester and Milford.

From the car park go left on the Ystwyth Trail, heading south. Here the trail uses the old line, which was opened in 1866. It

◄ Ponies grazing at Cors Caron

took a feat of engineering to get it over the bog; track was laid on a causeway sitting on a bed of wood and wool.

The embankment gives a good view across the bog to the hills to the west. After about 1km pass the wooden arch on your right and continue along the trail until you reach a second arch, which has been made from living willow.

Go through the arch to emerge onto the boardwalk. On either side you will see areas of moss-filled water with drier patches that have heather and cotton grass growing on them. In wetter parts you may be able to spot sundews. The small carnivorous plants have sticky, red leaves to trap small insects.

When you reach a junction in the boardwalk go left to reach the observatory, which is a good place to look out for birds. About 70 different species breed on or near the reserve, including curlew and redshank.

From the observatory, retrace your steps to the boardwalk junction and go left. The open water areas you pass are holes that were cut when peat was dug from the bog, now being reclaimed by nature.

In time the boardwalk returns you to the Ystwyth Trail at the wooden arch. Go left to return to your starting point at the car park.

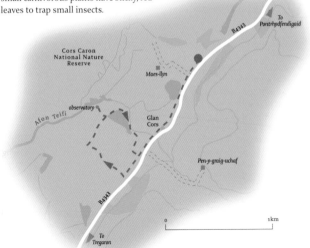

Strata Florida

Distance **4km** Time **1 hour 30**
Terrain **footpath and roads**
Map **OS Explorer 187** Access **bus (T21) from
Aberystwyth to Pontrhydfendigaid**

**Tucked into surrounding hills,
atmospheric Strata Florida Abbey is
peaceful and remote, but it was once a
centre of power in the long struggle
between the Anglo-Normans and the
native Welsh.**

This is a walk that is best combined
with a look around the abbey. It has a
fascinating story to tell – one that's eight
centuries long. It began when monks
from Whitland Abbey, near Carmarthen,

set off for the wild heart of what is now
Ceredigion to establish a new monastery.
They chose a location described as being
'far removed from the concourse of men'.

That abbey is thought to have been
built by a stream called the Afon Fflur on
land claimed by a powerful Norman lord.
But soon after the abbey was set up, the
lord's fortunes changed when he was
captured by the Lord Rhys, an influential
Welsh leader. The power shift threatened
the monastery, but the Lord Rhys became
its new patron.

The abbey's name needs some
explanation. Soon after its creation it was
relocated, but its name survived the
move. So, the abbey known as Ystrad Fflur

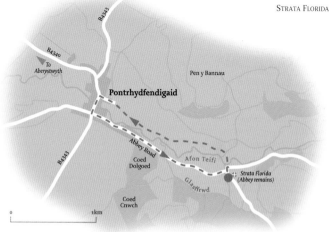

in Welsh, or Strata Florida in Latin, is on the Teifi not the Fflur.

Start your walk at the abbey after having a look around the ruins and visitor centre (which offers tea and coffee). The quality of the masonry of the abbey's huge carved west doorway gives a sense of how impressive the building must have been, and decorated floor tiles hint at luxury.

From the churchyard gate, head away from the abbey to the road junction. There go right and then climb over a stile on the left into a riverside field.

Cross the field to a footbridge, heading straight across the next field to a stile by the riverbank. Follow the path along the valley close to the fast-flowing Teifi.

On the way you pass the remains of an old lead mine, one of many that once operated in the area, and cross a series of waymarked stiles at each field boundary. The landmark hill to the north is Pen y

Bannau. Inhabitants of its Iron Age hillfort must have had commanding views of their lands from its 352m summit.

The first indication that you're getting close to Pontrhydfendigaid comes when you see the buildings of Dolebolion farm on your right. Soon you come to a stile into a large field, which is crossed by a series of telegraph poles.

Go diagonally across the field to the right of the poles to a stile in a fence. Go left along a lane to pass the Black Lion pub and arrive at the main road through the village.

Bear left along the road. You soon cross the bridge that gave the village its name – Pontrhydfendigaid translates as 'Bridge near the ford of the Blessed Virgin'.

At the first junction, go left into Abbey Road. It is a pleasant 20-minute walk along this lane to return to the abbey.

◀ Strata Florida Abbey's imposing west door

North of Aberystwyth the coastal strip between sea and mountains narrows. The flat land around the seaside community of Borth was once marshland, but most of it was drained long ago.

You'll see it best as you near the end of the scenic Aberystwyth-Borth coast walk. When you stand by the war memorial on the route's last hill, Borth, the Dyfi Estuary and the whole of the lowland strip are there to be 'read' like a map.

Borth's long beach is backed by the brown expanse of Borth Bog, where drainage channels run ruler-straight. In the far distance the giant sand dunes at Ynyslas mark the point where the Afon Dyfi flows to Cardigan Bay.

At the edge of this coastal plain there's a string of villages along the main Machynlleth road and then there's hills –

lots of them. Walks in this chapter at Cwm Einion, Tre Taliesin and Tal-y-bont take you along this upland edge, which makes for plenty of breathtaking views.

At Bont-goch you're way to the east, much further into the Cambrian Mountains. The route here uses old drovers' trails up into open country where you can be on the move all day without seeing another person, even on a Bank Holiday weekend.

The chapter ends on a high note with a walk to the top of Pumlumon Fawr, the very top of Mid Wales. This is a nursery for rivers – both the Severn and the Wye start out from the Pumlumon peaks – and is a walk that shouldn't be missed. The rock-strewn summit often sits under a cloud, but if you pick the right day you can see nearly all of Wales.

The sun sets over the war memorial at Upper Borth ▶

North of Aberystwyth

Coast Path to Borth

Distance 10.5km **Time** 3 hours (one way)
Terrain footpaths, steep in places, cliffs
Map OS Explorer 213 **Access** Aberystwyth
is well served by buses and trains; bus
(512) or train from Borth back to the start

**A Ceredigion Coast Path highlight, this is
a walk best bracketed by a train journey at
its beginning and end. Start out on
Aberystwyth's Cliff Railway and return by
train from Borth Railway Station.**

If you would rather walk up
Constitution Hill than ride, there's a path
on the left of the railway building that
zigzags up the hillside. It brings you to
the railway terminus, a café and other
buildings on the summit.

From here, bear left to find the Coast
Path, marked by a fingerpost. The path
keeps close to the clifftop, heading north.
After around 1.5km, it rounds the hillside
and you get your first view of Clarach Bay,
where the curved beach is backed by a
large caravan park. When the path comes
to a road, go left towards the beach.

The road crosses the valley just behind
the beach and brings you to a footbridge
over the Afon Clarach. Cross the bridge
and walk on past the beach café to a Coast
Path signpost.

Head up the hillside from here to reach
a kissing gate. Go through this and up
steps, then bear left along the Coast Path,
which runs close to the cliff edge.

For the next 2km or so the path is easy
to follow, a narrow strip between the
clifftop on one side and fences on the
right. In time you will be able to see a

◄ The Coast Path above Clarach Bay

stony spit called Sarn Gynfelyn (Saint Cynfelyn's Causeway), which runs dead-straight out into the bay at Wallog.

Old stories say that this spit was once a roadway that ran west to villages lost to the sea. In fact, the stones mark the course of an Ice Age glacier that ran along a valley here.

After passing in front of the large beachfront house, bear left to cross a bridge and climb straight up the slope ahead to a kissing gate. From Wallog the Coast Path rises and falls rollercoaster-style until you near the first of Borth's caravans.

Here, the path zigzags down toward a small bay. Bear left to cross a footbridge and then climb steps towards the war memorial ahead. This last ascent is a real test of stamina. When you reach the memorial, take a breather and enjoy the incredible views over the Dyfi Estuary to the mountains of Gwynedd. From the memorial the path drops down to a kissing gate, which opens onto Cliff Road. Walk the length of Cliff Road to a junction, where you go left.

If you are planning to return to Aberystwyth by bus, the stop is just across the road from the post office at the next junction. If you're travelling by train

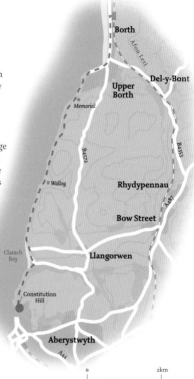

carry on along the village main street for 1km – the station is signed on the right.

Before you leave, take the time for a picnic and paddle at the beach. If you are lucky and the tide is out, you may see the stumps of a prehistoric forest that grew here before sea levels rose a the end of the last ice age.

83

Ynyslas Dunes

Distance **3km** Time **1 hour**
Terrain **paths, dunes and beach**
Map **OS Explorer 198** Access **bus (512) from
Aberystwyth to Ynyslas Turn, 1.75km
from the start**

**The Dyfi Estuary has a spectacular, wide
open feel. To the north, the mountains of
Snowdonia are an imposing backdrop to
the seaside community of Aberdyfi and at
low tide the expanse seems limitless.**

At Ynyslas the dynamics of sea and land
have created a barrier of huge sand dunes,
which this route takes you through.
Ynyslas is a National Nature Reserve and
this walk starts from its car park, which
overlooks a stretch of tidal sand called
Traeth Maelgwyn.

There's a legend that a 6th-century king,

Maelgwyn the Tall, once held a summit
meeting with rival kings at Traeth
Maelgwyn, giving the beach its name. It is
so open and flat that it would have made
an excellent place for enemies to meet if
they feared ambush.

From the noticeboard in the car park,
take the path west into the sand dunes.
You soon reach the reserve's visitor
centre, open from Easter to September.

Pass to the left of the centre to join a
path surfaced with crushed shells. It takes
you past dune slacks, low-lying areas that
become wet during the winter. In spring
look out for wild orchids that thrive in the
slacks, including the purple marsh orchid,
which flowers in June and July. In winter,
the mudflats and salt marshes of the Dyfi
Estuary provide sanctuary for the only

Map labels: Afon Dyfi, Traeth Maelgwyn, Twyni Bach, Visitor Centre, dunes, Afon Leri, Twyni Mawr, Ynys Tachwedd, Pont Aber Leri, Ynyslas, B4353, Borth Sands, B4353, 0 1km

known population of Greenland white-fronted geese in England and Wales.

In time, the path brings you to a wooden walkway and then a series of steps that climb to a viewpoint platform at the summit. On a clear, sharp day the 360-degree panorama is spectacular. The route then continues along the walkway before dropping down to the beach. There's a fascinating coming together of folklore and fact along this stretch of the Ceredigion coast.

An old story tells of a time when what is now Cardigan Bay was an area of low-lying farmland called Cantref Gwaelod (the Lowland Hundred). It is said that a mishap with gates in a sea wall led to the lowland being inundated by the sea. True enough, sea levels did rise sharply after the last ice age and at Ynyslas a forest was flooded. After winter storms at low tide, the stumps of drowned trees can sometimes be seen between Ynyslas and Borth.

At the high tide line go right to walk along the beach. At the red warning flag there's a choice of routes. For a longer walk keep following the high tide line around the end of the headland (this adds around 1.5km/30 minutes to the walk).

Along the way you'll pass a pole that marks the point where passengers used to embark on a ferry that shuttled travellers across to the other side of the river. Soon after you will arrive back at the car park.

Alternatively, go right at the flag to take the path that climbs into the dunes. It's quite a slog in the fine sand and a real test for your calf muscles. At the crest of the slope follow the marked path, which soon takes you back to your start point.

◀ Approaching the beach from the dunes at Ynyslas

Tal-y-bont heritage loop

Distance **3.6km** Time **1 hour**
Terrain **minor roads and footpaths**
Map **OS Explorer 213** Access **bus (X28) from
Aberystwyth to Tal-y-bont**

**Enjoy views to the coast and mountains
on this short tour of a little village that
was once a mining 'boom town' with many
listed buildings and two attractive pubs.**

Mining has played a big part in Tal-y-bont's past. Silver and lead were being
mined at Tal-y-bont way back in the 17th
century, but the village's mining boom
happened in the late 19th century.

By the 1870s most local men were either
miners or worked in a trade that served
the mines, such as carpentry or
metalwork. Some Tal-y-bont miners even

traded their skills elsewhere in the
county, coming home at weekends to
collect their wages at the Black Lion pub,
one of two pubs on the village green.

But the boom years came to an end and
the last of the mines closed just before
the First World War. Many Tal-y-bont
miners moved away to work in the pits of
South Wales or further afield; one globe-
trotting miner ended up working in the
USA, Russia and South America.

The village green is the start point for
this walk. From the green, cross the main
road and head out of the village along
Ceulan Terrace opposite.

Keep left at the junction to climb uphill.
The wooded hill ahead is Allt y Crib, which
was the scene of much of the mining

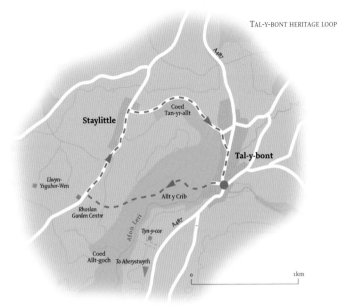

activity at Tal-y-bont. One deep horizontal shaft that dates from the mid-1800s actually runs below the village main street for half a mile into the heart of Allt y Crib.

At a gate, go left and stay on the path to a junction with a waymark post. Here, go right and carry on through the woods.

When you come to a track cross over and take the path to the right, which carries on uphill. In time you'll come to a junction of four paths – go straight on to pass a waymark post.

The path takes you to a stile at the edge of the wood. Climb over and go left to walk around the perimeter of a large field. In time you'll be treated to views to the coast at Borth and, on a clear day, you may be able to make out the mountains

of Snowdonia to the north.

Walk to the gate and along the hedgeline to a stile. Cross the stile onto a minor road and go right to walk about 1km to the hamlet of Staylittle. Continue through Staylittle to a road junction, where you turn right.

This lane takes you around the shoulder of the hill and back towards Tal-y-bont. When you reach a Y-junction on the edge of the village keep right to walk along a lane that soon brings you to the A487.

Go right to return along the village's main street to the green. Along the way you will pass some of the fine 19th-century buildings that date from the village's mining heyday, including the Bethel Chapel and the Tabernacl.

◀ One of Tal-y-bont's many chapels

Tre Taliesin and the bard's grave

Distance 5.5km Time 1 hour 30
Terrain paths, bridleways and roads; steep
in parts Map OS Explorer OL23 Access bus
(X28) from Aberystwyth to Tre Taliesin

**This is a walk for poets and prospectors.
Romans came looking for lead in the
country around Tre Taliesin and it is also
said to be the last resting place of one of
Wales' greatest bards.**

Like other villages in north Ceredigion,
Tre Taliesin is said to have been an
outpost of Roman power who, it is
claimed, came here to mine lead ore close
to 2000 years ago. Part of the village is still
called The Romans, which may or may not
give credence to the claim.

This walk takes you away from the
village and up into the wooded hills,
where there were more recent mines.

Drivers can park in a lay-by just north of
the village. From here, walk south

through the village, passing the school, to
reach a footpath sign that points the way
left to a gap through the houses.

The road ends at a bungalow, so bear
right up steps to a narrow path that runs
behind gardens to meet a track. Cross this
and go left on a footpath that rises
towards the woodland ahead.

When you reach a path T-junction, turn
left, going right at a fork after about 50m
to keep rising through the woods.

Cross straight over a woodland track to
take the waymarked path ahead. Climb
over one stile and carry straight on to a
second, where you should bear right to
follow the fenceline past mining spoil.

Carry on up the valley, keeping to the
right to a waymark at the woodland edge.
From here, continue straight on to pass to
the left of a ruined building.

Go through a gate and straight on along
the hedgeline, passing a farm. When the

◄ A capstone marks
Bedd Taliesin –
Taliesin's grave

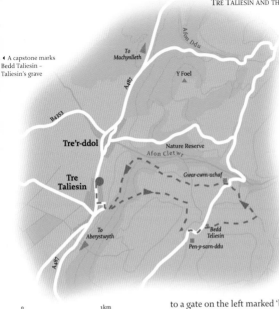

To
Machynlleth

Afon Ddu

Y Foel

A487

B4353

Tre'r-ddol

Nature Reserve

Afon Clettwr

Gwar-cwm-uchaf

Tre
Taliesin

To
Aberystwyth

Bedd
Teliesin

Pen-y-sarn-ddu

A487

0   1km

path reaches the farm track, go right and continue to a gate on the left.

Pass through the gate and onto a minor road. Keep left and walk on until you come to a gate across the road. Instead of passing through it, go right – after about 30m you come to Bedd Taliesin.

This stone-capped grave is thought to date from the Bronze Age, but traditionally it is linked with the 6th-century poet Taliesin. The leading bard of his day, he wrote poems in praise of rulers throughout Britain.

Head on along the lane until you come

to a gate on the left marked 'bridleway'. Take the bridleway to meet a gate that opens onto a minor road.

Turn left along the road to reach the nearby house, then right at the signposted bridleway. Go straight on down the hillside until you come to a gate into woodland.

The path then zigzags down through Cwm Clettwr, which is a nature reserve. At the reserve gate go left on a path that passes a stable and joins a track.

Carry straight on to a path on the right that drops down a flight of steps. The route then runs along the woodland edge until you arrive back at the outward path from the village.

The Artists' Valley

Distance **2.5km** Time **1 hour**
Terrain **roads, paths and bridleways; some
steep stretches** Map **OS Explorer OL23**
Access **bus (X28) from Aberystwyth to
Machynlleth stops at Furnace**

**Sometimes known as the Artists' Valley
and said to have attracted landscape
painters in the 19th century, Cwm Einion
is a real gem. It has an out-of-the-way feel
and is a tranquil place to walk, even on a
Bank Holiday weekend.**

Furnace was once at the cutting edge of
technological development. In the late
18th century this hamlet was a centre for
iron-making that used the latest
techniques to smelt ore from northern
England using Welsh charcoal.

Take a few minutes to look around the
furnace building, which stands next to
the main Aberystwyth road by the Einion.

As it turned out, the iron business
failed – the waterwheel you can see
today dates from a time when the building
was a sawmill.

If arriving by car, the furnace car park is
just off the A487 and is well signposted.
This walk starts from the furnace, turning
right at the gate to cross the bridge and
head north along the main road.

After 100m turn right to take a narrow
lane that passes some houses before rising
into woodland. You can soon hear the
sound of the waterfall at the furnace,
which is close by on the right.

Carry on along the lane, which soon
crosses a cattle grid and zigzags up the
flank of Foel Fawr. As the road climbs,
there are impressive views to Borth and
north to the Dyfi and mountains.

Follow the road along the valley side
until you reach a bridleway, which drops

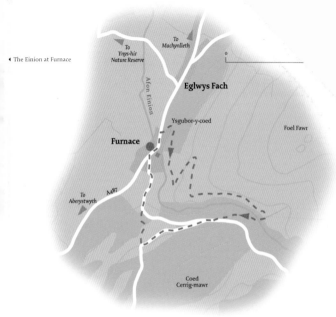

◀ The Einion at Furnace

To Machynlleth

To Ynys-hir Nature Reserve

Eglwys Fach

Afon Einion

Ysgubor-y-coed

Foel Fawr

Furnace

A487

To Aberystwyth

Coed Cerrig-mawr

down from the road to the right. It is marked by a fingerpost and a nearby sign reads 'Felin y Cwm'.

Where the bridleway comes to a cottage go through the gate on the right, which is marked 'Wales Coast Path'. Take the path down to the river and then cross over the bigger of two footbridges, which is on the right.

From the footbridge, the path takes you up through conifer woodland and on to a minor road. Turn right and after around 50m take the footpath on the left, again signposted 'Wales Coast Path'.

The track takes you along the edge of the woodland to a junction of five paths by a fingerpost. Take the path on your right, which is steep and narrow.

At the road, go left. There's a chance that you're now walking on Sarn Helen, a Roman road which ran through the heart of Ceredigion linking forts on the outer edge of the Roman Empire – one was at Erglodd, just a few miles south of Furnace.

The exact line of Sarn Helen is unknown, but it is thought that it may have run along the southern side of Cwm Einion to a bridge, or ford, at Furnace. Roman or not, this stage lasts just 300m until you're back at the A487 and your start point.

...ont-goch

...30

...s; can be

Access no public transport to the start

You can spend all day walking the rolling hills above Bont-goch without meeting a single person. But you will find plenty of clues that point to a time when these hills were a hive of activity, as this was once the heart of lead mining country.

Park in the heart of the village close to St Peter's Church and head northeast on the road away from the village centre.

When it comes to a lone farm shed, look out for a bridleway sign close by on your right. Go through a gate and follow the fenceline, passing the shed and heading

uphill on Banc Bwlch Rosser. As you gain height, you have good views west to the sea. In the valley below are ruined buildings, a reminder of the area's industrial past.

There were once many lead mines around Bont-goch, the oldest thought to date back to the early 1600s. The mines were big employers and most of the buildings in the village date from the industry's heyday in the mid-19th century.

Carry on along the fence for more than 1km until the path drops down to a gate. Go through the gate and bear left to a small stream, which has to be forded.

Ahead, pass through an iron gate and bear right. Go through the next field gate and follow the bridleway up the hillside –

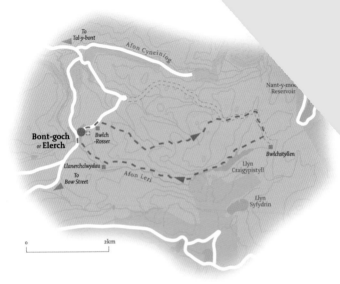

it is marked by a line of gorse bushes.

After a while, you come to two field gates; go through both gates and then climb towards the pass ahead. For a time you're walking above a track on the left. Where the routes converge, carry straight on to drop down to a flat marshy area.

When the track comes to a three-way junction, turn right. Around 500m further on you approach a gate at a ford. Don't go through this gate; instead take the path on the right towards Llyn Craigypistyll.

The path crosses the hillside parallel with the shore of the reservoir until it drops down to the dam where a narrow path takes you on through the gorge. High on the steep valley side, the path follows the course of the Afon Leri, where it drops

through a series of waterfalls. Walk towards a footbridge, but don't cross it; instead stay on the path along the valley.

Keep right when the paths split. Then, further on, where the track begins to climb away from the river, bear left to stay close to the Leri.

In time, when the track drops back nearer to the river, rejoin it and head straight on. Where the track approaches a farm, leave it again to bear right onto a waymarked path that soon comes to a gate onto the farm track.

Here, go right and carry on along the valley to a minor road into the village. Turn right and walk along the road to a junction, where you turn right again to return to the village church.

◀ The path high above the Afon Leri

er 213
:o
1

At 752m, Pumlumon is Mid Wales' highest mountain and close by are the sources of the Rivers Wye and Severn. On a good day you can see both Snowdonia and the Brecon Beacons from the summit.

The Pumlumon massif dominates the north of Ceredigion, and Pen Pumlumon Fawr is its high point, the tallest of the massif's five peaks. It's tough country – and can be bleak – but if you like wilderness, you'll love the peace and sense of space.

The start point for this walk is a group of farm buildings at Eisteddfa Gurig on the north side of the busy A44. You can park your car in the farmyard for £3 per day, or if there is no space there's a lay-by 500m further on along the A44, just beyond the Powys border sign.

If you opt for the bus instead ask for the Eisteddfa Gurig stop, which is sometimes known as The Elvis Stone. A large roadside rock just beyond the hamlet has the name 'Elvis' painted on it.

From the parking area just off the road, go left into the farmyard and then right to a gate marked 'All Walks', which opens onto a track.

It is now a steady slog along what was once a miners' track for close to 2km. In

time you reach evidence of the old mineworkings just off the track on the banks of the Afon Tarennig.

A little further on at a waymark post, the track bears right and the Pumlumon path leaves it on the left. The path strikes out across the hillside and is marked at first by weathered wooden posts and, later, by small cairns.

As you near the summit you come to a sheep fence that runs north to south. Cross the fence at the stile, then walk to the trig point that marks the very top of Pumlumon Fawr. At the summit you can appreciate the wild landscape of the Cambrian Mountains. It's easy to see why the area is sometimes called the Green Desert of Wales.

In legend, the knights Cai and Bedwyr watched from Pumlumon 'in the highest wind that ever was in the world' for the giant Dillus Farfog. And the hills made a perfect hideout, too, for the forces of Owain Glyndwr during his 15th-century rebellion against English rule.

After enjoying the view, go back to the stile and climb to the far side of the fence. Then turn right to drop downhill, keeping the fence on your right.

As you descend, keep close to the fence until you near a forestry plantation ahead. Close to the plantation the path bears left to join a track, which continues downhill along the plantation edge.

Shortly after passing a pylon, you'll come to a track intersecting your path to enter the plantation. Go left to take this track away from the trees, snaking back down to Eisteddfa Gurig.

◄ Mist closes in at the summit of Pen Pumlumon Fawr

95

Index